Social Theory and Aging

Jason L. Powell

ROWMAN & LITTLEFIELD PUBLISHERS, INC.
Lanham • Boulder • New York • Toronto • Oxford

ROWMAN & LITTLEFIELD PUBLISHERS, INC.

Published in the United States of America
by Rowman & Littlefield Publishers, Inc.
A wholly owned subsidiary of The Rowman & Littlefield Publishing Group, Inc.
4501 Forbes Boulevard, Suite 200, Lanham, Maryland 20706
www.rowmanlittlefield.com

PO Box 317
Oxford
OX2 9RU, UK

British Library Cataloguing in Publication Information Available

Library of Congress Cataloging-in-Publication Data

Powell, Jason L., 1971–
  Social theory and aging / Jason L. Powell.
    p. cm.
  Includes bibliographical references and index.
  ISBN 0-7425-1953-8 (cloth : alk. paper) — ISBN 0-7425-1954-6 (pbk. : alk.
paper)
  1. Gerontology—Philosophy. 2. Aging. 3. Postmodernism. I. Title.
HQ1061.P684 2005
305.26'01—dc22   2005017316

Printed in the United States of America

∞™ The paper used in this publication meets the minimum requirements of
American National Standard for Information Sciences—Permanence of Paper for
Printed Library Materials, ANSI/NISO Z39.48-1992.

Contents

Series Editor's Foreword

Charles Lemert

We, if you will pardon the expression, who practice the art of social theory owe this activity of our adult lives to global transformation that began, for many of us, in our youth. Some of us are old enough to have lived and worked through the world revolution of 1968 and all that came before and issued there from.

In those days, had we investigated what was going on in the academy (as few of us did) we would have not found the expression "social theory" used so often or with such intensity as it is today. The expression was there, but not the practices to which today it refers.

What social theory came to be, as both an academic and secular practice, is something much more akin to the wild generative ideas of the global 1960s than the pale pure science of formal academic theories in various disciplinary fields. In those days, the writings and speeches of Frantz Fanon, C. Wright Mills, Simone de Beauvoir, Herbert Marcuse, and Malcolm X, among many others, supplied the inspiration for rethinking the world then changing as today it still is, beyond anything we who were young in those days could have imagined.

Social theory as it is practiced today was not of course purely and simply a political thing. With rare exception the political figures of the revolutionary 60s either academics descending into the streets (like Marcuse) or the self-selected voices of those who suffered in the alleys off the barricaded streets (like de Beauvoir and Malcolm). Whether fully certified as

Marcuse or self-taught as Malcolm, those figures were global thinkers because they were daring enough to engage the world as it was—or, in ret-
rospect, as it was ceasing to be. They did not so much cause the changes
that overwhelm us today as see them coming and understand the justice
of it all. Social theory trades in justice-denied in order to think through the
possibilities for its renewal.

Had Malcolm, who was assassinated in 1964, and Fanon, who died of
cancer in 1961, lived to the new century we are most uncomfortably in,
they would have both been 80 years old in 2005—old men by any reck-
oning. Had Mills survived the heart attack that killed him in 1962, he
would have been 89—an age beyond the fondest wishes of anyone
whose system was so damaged by acute physical stress aggravated by a
frenetic life style. Though those who sparked the revolutions that spread
around the world in 1968 were of course supplanted by, now, several
generations of social theorists, they rest where we must stand.

It would not be outrageous, thus, to say that social theory itself is
aging—an old person's game. When played by the young it is nonethe-
less played in hands dealt in the long ago. This may be why a great deal
of social theory seems so awkward to those who found the revolution of
1968 terrifying or who were reared by parents who did or otherwise
bought the nostalgic agenda that fights on today to turn back the clock to
the golden age with men were brave and lay only with women they called
girls, while all the others kept quiet.

Jason Powell's *Social Theory and Aging* is elixir for those then not afraid
as it would be cathartic for those who were and are. If social theory, an
invention of the once young, can age with the ideas that began it all, then
naturally it must accept in the passing of time the reality of aging itself as
both a resource and a topic. Powell's wonderful book accepts this fact of
the human body and the collective history by bringing to the subject of
aging the wisdom of those who, had they lived, would have been themselves quite aged. Foucault, one of Powell's most important resources,
who died of AIDS in 1984, was born in 1924, the year before Fanon and
Mills. One can hardly imagine his most strikingly beautiful visage and vi-
brant body worn and wrinkled with age. We who share Powell's respect
for him, as for the others, remember him as a young man—as (not inci-
dentally) we remember ourselves. Someone old and fading once re-
marked that whenever he looked in the mirror he wondered what he was
doing in that decrepit body. This is but one of the themes Powell ad-

dresses with honest insight—the figure of the postmodern body which, I would add, still resists its Unthinkable age.

There are many more ways *Social Theory and Aging* brings us up against the reality of time, which may be wisdom but cannot be that without also being a ghost of some former self. Powell writes with a better urgency than those who sponsor the idea of risk society of the dangers attendant to reality such as it is, which is always and necessarily out of time with its origins. Many readers will recognize behind the scene of Powell's discourse the most original idea of Foucault's French generation: that the principle of origins is the base ideology of progressive history with its absurd expectation of unending growth that denies the reality of limits—of which no limit more real than age and death. At the same time those who regard the French of that time as the evil empire of all that is wrong with our age will, if they overcome their fear, profit from this book because, its sources and languages aside, it is such a straight-on essay on this one reality we all face.

Who is not aging? Who among us will not die? Yet, who apart from those already under sentence of the day of their death, does not pretend that the body in the mirror is that of a stranger who has taken hold the young soul we long still to be? There may be exceptions to these rules. They will not find much here from which to learn. *Social Theory and Aging* is, thus, for anyone who has the courage to accept aging, the wisdom to face death, and serenity to live in the between.

Acknowledgments

I would like to thank Rowman & Littlefield for their help and patience in the development of this book. It has been a journey through which I must give Alan McClare and Professor Charles Lemert profound thanks for their staunch support and advice.

There are so many people who have helped shape my ideas over the past few years. Firstly, the genius of Michel Foucault inspired my critical thoughts on "debunking" gerontology. It was once stated that Foucault's concepts are fired like arrows into air only to be caught by Foucauldian-inspired theorists and taken in a new trajectory—in this instance, the gerontology trajectory, by this inspired Foucauldian!

I have swapped important ideas concerning "social theory and aging" with many collaborators whose contribution I would like to acknowledge: Professor Simon Biggs for his critical insights and kind friendship; Dr. Azrini Wahidin for warm camaraderie and fantastic support; and Professor Charles F. Longino Jr., for his wonderful encouragement and sheer inspiration. I would also like to thank Joe Sim, Marion Price, Margaret Edwards, Ian Cook, Steve Jackson, Richard Jenkins, John Lansley, Harry R. Moody, Tim May, and Chris Phillipson for their conversations and supportive advice of the past few years.

I would also like to thank my friends Howard Vane, Dave Popham, Gerard Delanty, Mel Walker, Rob Morris, Steve Lawler, Peter Millward, Moira Rangel, and Steve Miles for their support. Lastly, I would also like to thank my family: my Mum and Martyn, Rebekah, and Angela; my Grandad; Eddie Cropper Jr.; and "Zack," "Bonnie," "Mickey," and "Soothie." My partner Stella Powell has been a profound influence to me, and this shines through on every page; a wonderful partner.

In particular, without my Grandad's magnificent support, many of the ideas in this book would never have been realized. It is for that reason that I dedicate this book to him.

1

The Relationship of Social Theory and Aging

A Critical Exegesis

[handwritten annotation: an explanation — critical interpretation]

INTRODUCTION

This book explores both conceptual and theoretical issues that impinge on understanding aging in (post) modern society. It analyzes how knowledge formation of aging, with particular reference to "old age" in contemporary Western society, is socially constituted and positioned by powerful, taken-for-granted assumptions. These assumptions have provided a power/knowledge base for biomedical disciplines, the legitimacy of political-economic discourses, and the practices of professional experts.

Given this objective, the book explores theoretical issues about the ontological status of knowledge, examining and moving beyond conventional biomedical philosophical dualisms of "aging as decline"/"decline as aging." Indeed, Michel Foucault's (1977) notion that we are governed by means of *social processes* by which we affirm our freedom is highly pertinent. The informed use of "thinking tools" from social theory is part of the epistemic aim to debunk and shatter those taken-for-granted assumptions about constructions of aging, its biomedical contestations, and theoretical relationships of macro/micro and object/subject to issues of culture, body, power/knowledge, and risk.

The book is in two parts. The first part introduces "modernist" scientific models and theories of gerontology and questions their importance in mapping out the assumptions of aging and how they impinge on

1

identity performance in society through a disciplinary matrix of biology, psychology, and social conceptualizations of gerontology; the second part focuses upon "postmodern" constructions of aging through the articulation and development of novel epistemologies: postmodernism and aging body; discourse and power/knowledge; and "aging" in the "risk society."

Indeed, the book addresses a key question: can "meta-theories" provide an effective analysis of aging that is radically different from modernist "grand narratives" as epitomized not only by biomedical models of aging but also by mainstream social theories of gerontology inclusive of modernist epistemes of Functionalist theories of activity and disengagement, feminist gerontology, and the political economy of old age?

The critically acclaimed sociologist C. Wright Mills, in *The Sociological Imagination* (1959), powerfully illustrates that the sociologist seeks, first, to understand the relationship of personal troubles and public issues and the intersection of biography and history; then, these polarities, and the ways in which sociologists address them, define the central problems of social theory in modernity. Mills further argues that the role of the sociologist is to reveal the connections between what is going on in the world and what may be happening within ourselves—in other words, "to grasp history and biography and the relations between the two within society." Mills believed that sociologists develop a quality of mind that enables them to show individuals how their own private troubles may be linked to features of the "public world" of modernity.

Modernity itself was both a "war of liberation" and a "war against mystery and magic" (Bauman 1992, x). It was thought that the world should be despiritualized and instead replaced with "Big Science" (Bauman 1992, x). The "master narrative" of "progress" became the new "God," "rational" replaced "irrational," and truth became the new "mission." In modernity the ultimate goals of progress and the mastery of nature became assumed and unquestioned, just as God had gone unquestioned in religious faith (Bauman 1992, xiv). Zygmunt Bauman has suggested that a distinguishing characteristic of modernity was the desperate search for a structured world, in which a search for social facts—such as the ways in which individuals come together in societies through a "social contract," or the ways in which "social facts" may determine individual behavior—continue to be debated along with newer concerns with levels of analysis, freedom, determinism, and morality.

Indeed, in recent years the German philosopher Jürgen Habermas (1992) has presented us with the doctrine of *dialogical morality* in modernity, which suggests that the identification of freedom must be arrived at collectively by all those agents likely to be affected by its adoption.

As a rival to the modernist preoccupation with macro grand narratives of "progress" and "reason," postmodernism became increasingly fashionable in its epistemological war against grand narratives. It brought with it an "anything goes" *social context* "which renounces purity, mastery of form and elitism and is more playful, ironic and eclectic in style" (Thompson 1992, 227).

Postmodernism not only affects culture but also impinges on a range of developments in all areas of Western society, such as politics, industry, and the media and the rise of social movements, ultimately leading to the development of a postmodern world characterized by "fragmentation, multiplicity, plurality and indeterminacy" (Thompson 1992, 223). If this characterization is correct, it has had strong implications for the Enlightenment aims and values of modernist approaches of social theory. It is the acceptance that modern aims of universalism are futile and the recognition of "pluralism of cultures, communal traditions, ideologies, 'forms of life' or 'language games'" (Bauman 1992, 102). Whereas for modernists such as Habermas (1992) universalism of collective action is central to determine social change in a social world, for postmodernism (Powell and Longino 2001) microprocesses of individualization, subjectification, and risk are part of fragmented social spaces, through which identities are formed and performed, that will run counter to macro processes.

Henceforth, the interpretation of the positioning of aging as macro- and fixed explanations or micro- and fluid existentialism lies at the heart of modern-postmodern debates within contemporary culture that are plugged into a contestation of "aging"—how is aging defined? What constitutes the aging process? How relevant is science in its understanding? This demands interrogation from transparent theoretical perspectives.

Clearly, what is striking is that one of the major problems of understanding aging in recent years is that it has evidently not been directed by social theory (Powell and Longino 2002). Indeed, theoretical innovations in gerontology have, according to Vern L. Bengston and colleagues (1997) lagged well behind other sociological master narratives of race, class, and

gender. Linda George (1995, 77) consolidates this by claiming that gerontological research has been "theoretically sterile." For example, in a study
of published refereed articles in eight leading North American gerontology journals (as listed in the Social Science Citation Index) from 1990 to
1995, Bengston and colleagues (1997) claimed that 80 percent of the refereed articles lacked a theoretical framework. Bengston and colleagues
(1997) further argue that social gerontology, a dimension of gerontology,
has been "itty-bitty" in its development of theoretical frameworks to assist
an understanding of an important issue such as aging: ". . . it is intellectu-
ally irresponsible for a program of research to proceed without . . . a theory" (Bengston, Burgess, and Parrot 1997, 73).

Ironically, part of the problem about lack of social theory in the study
of aging relates to the field of gerontology itself. Gerontology as a *scientific discipline* has been dominated with a preoccupation with biomedical
sciences and its constituent elements of "decline" models of biology and
psychology (Estes and Binney 1989; Longino and Powell 2004). Gerontology based on *social theories of aging* sees aging as a socially constructed category with differential epistemological prisms: for example,
functionalism and feminist gerontology. However, while both definitions
are fundamental to the complexities of aging in the social world, the theoretical interpretations of aging are in their "infancy" (Estes, Biggs, and
Phillipson 2003).

If we take the disciplinary dimensions of gerontology, we can illuminate both the relevance and importance they have for understanding the
social constructions of aging, as well as raising questions about the development of theorizing from wider social theory. We can suggest that
gerontology has two focal points in its broad conceptualization: (1)
gerontology as science and (2) gerontology as social theory.

Gerontology as "Science"

One of the cornerstones of modern gerontology has been a belief in
"science" and "progress" as constituting "discursive practices that give
rise to epistemological figures, sciences and possibly formalised systems" (Foucault 1972, 191). Such powerful discourses systematize networks of ideas about the "nature" of aging, the reasons for particular behaviors, and the ways individuals may be classified, selected, and
controlled (Biggs and Powell 2001). The "project of modernity" has inspired the disciplinary development of gerontology to reconstruct aging

on the basis of individual abilities, needs, and functions. The aging subject is constructed as an object of knowledge and as a seeker of that knowledge. This tension gives gerontology its character. On the one hand, it produces the subject as an empirically verifiable entity, and on the other, it produces a critical inquiry into the empirical conditions that justify the existence of subjects. Hence, we get a developmental duality of an empirical and transcendental entity. Indeed, knowledge formation in Western gerontology in particular, is modeled and characterized by quantitative, positivist, and scientific discourses (Katz 1996; Powell 2001b; Biggs and Powell 2001; Powell and Biggs 2000; Powell 2002; Longino and Powell 2004). Traditional forms of medical-scientific expertise and knowledge under the rubric of the "biomedical model" have attempted to foster understanding of aging and construct "worldview" "truths" about aging that are perceived as "master narratives" (Powell 2001b). Master narratives are dense forms of discourse containing alleged universal truths, totalizing views and symbols with which to explain and understand almost every aspect of social life. These narratives play a central role in the construction of physical and symbolic boundaries, and it is through them that social groups come to know and understand the social world and constitute the classification of perceived aging identities (Biggs and Powell 2001).

Such scientific narratives construct a particular positioning of aging. For example, Bytheway (1995) suggests the notion of "growth" is a central scientific discourse relating to the true changes to the biological body associated with human aging. Growth is seen as a positive development by biologists (Bytheway 1995) in that a baby grows into a child who grows into an adult, but then, instead of *growing* into old age, the person *declines*. This scientific sanctioned perception is that growth slows when a person reaches "old age" and is subsequently interpreted as decline rather than as change, which is taken for granted with earlier life-course transitions. These narratives can be understood as textual formations composed by a complex set of truth codes and conventions through which scientifically grounded and privileged forms of true knowledge strive to present their worldviews as universal and hence valid for the whole of society.

Hence, aging is a site upon which *power games* are played out mainly through such narratives. As Biggs and Powell point out: ". . . narratives are not simply personal fictions that we choose to live by, but are discourses that are subject to social and historical influence" (2001, 113).

Coupled with this, the totalizing views of biomedical science, as Longino and Powell (2004) have pointed out, make a particular representation of the world seem so natural that aging, for example, cannot be imagined as an alternative discourse except as an abnormality that can be understood only through biomedical science.

However, the objectivity and neutrality of scientific knowledge expressed in broad approaches such as the biomedical model can be understood as rhetorical surfaces that obscure subterranean, politically structured orders. Coupled with this, it has become increasingly clear that a "scientific" knowledge formation lacks appropriate language for discussing theoretical and philosophical concerns or appreciating their historical and contemporary cultural contexts (Kastenbaum 1993). Therefore, as Katz (1996) has identified, aging is not just a scientific process, and for this reason it cannot be singularly analyzed via "disciplines" such as "biomedical gerontology." Furthermore, according to Katz (1996, 55), the effects of the "decline" analogy can be seen in the dominance of biomedical arguments about the physiological "problems" of the "aging body." Indeed, the master narrative of biological decline hides the location of a complex web of intersections of negative ideas constituting a culture of aging (Powell 2001c). Coupled with this, Foucault suggests that the surveillance of bodies was central to the development of modern regimes of power and knowledge or what Estes (1979) calls "aging enterprises"—which are institutions created to manage the "problems" of aging, from social services to nursing care through to social work with older people (Powell and Biggs 2003). Katz (1996, 27) asks: "How . . . was the figure of the aged body central to the modern constitution of old age and development of *biomedical* knowledge?" (emphasis in original).

We address this in chapter 2 with an eliciting of scientific assumptions, but it is a question constantly reflected upon throughout the book. The biomedical model is a powerful discipline and practice, but for Powell and Biggs, it obscures wider understanding of gerontology:

> It appears . . . that established and emerging "master narratives" of biological decline yet linked through the importance of techniques for maintenance . . . via medicalized bodily control. However, this focus on medicalization . . . has tended to obscure another . . . discourse on aging . . . the association between old age and social *theory* [*emphasis in original*]. (2000, 95)

Gerontology as Social Theory

The theoretical concerns of positivist biomedical disciplinarity have significant implications for the social discourses that impinge upon the social construction of aging. How have these social discourses and policy implications been interpreted via social theories of gerontology?

A striking feature of theoretical frameworks of aging is that the majority of studies are relatively small in scale (Moody 1998). Despite Functionalist (Cumming and Henry 1961), Marxist (Phillipson 1982, 1998; Walker 1981), feminist (Arber and Ginn 1995) and "postmodern" (Featherstone and Wernick 1995; Gilleard and Higgs 2000) forms of gerontological analysis, gerontology has remained "theoretically sterile" in comparison with other social science disciplines such as political science and criminology (George 1995); as an apparently "applied" field of gerontological study it has remained "itty-bitty" (Bengston, Burgess, and Parrot 1997) in theorizing aging. Bengston and Schaie (1999) also claim that theoretical developments in gerontology have at best a limited history (1999, 41). Katz (1996, 42) consolidates this by claiming that the use of aging in ways that are informed by the cultivation of *wider* social theories of postmodernism and Foucauldian studies, for example, is relatively unknown territory.

In order to add and develop the relationship of aging and contemporary social theory in an area left "uncharted," this book contributes to, and strengthens, the critical interconnection between aging and contemporary social theories of aging body, power/knowledge, discourse, and subjectivity and risk. While, for example, postmodernism, Foucauldian theory, and risk are challenging other disciplinary fields in social science, mainstream social gerontology is impermeable (Estes, Biggs, and Phillipson 2003). Surrounded by its biomedical paradigms, gerontology fails to recognize that its most imaginative developments come from the critical and cutting edge theories of those scholars who transcend so-called fixed disciplinary boundaries. It is therefore timely that this book is written when serious questions (Phillipson 1998; George 1995; Bengston, Burgess, and Parrot 1997; and Biggs 1999) are being raised about the limited development of wider social theory in social gerontology.

Despite this, the "biomedical" study of aging has dominated the disciplinary development of gerontology which has masked the historical development in theorizing aging (Katz 1996). The biomedical model problematizes aging as a pathological "problem" tied to discourses of "decline," "dependency," "decay," "abnormality," and "deterioration" (Powell 2002). Thus, the problem orientation to aging is historically configured in biomedical sciences and discourses that specialize in the medical reductionism of gerontology (Powell 2001a; Powell and Biggs 2000; Biggs and Powell 2001). As Foucault pointed out: "It [is] a matter of analyzing . . . the problematizations through which being offers itself to be, necessarily, thought—and the practices on the basis of which these problematizations are formed" (Foucault 1977, 11).

The biomedical problematization of aging has secreted wider questions of power, inequality, and culture, and the growth in "social aspects" of aging has developed as a direct challenge to the authority of biomedical power and knowledge. The purpose of this book is not only to challenge such knowledge formation but also to map out the terrain of evocative modern and postmodern theories and their contestations and insights for understanding aging. It has only been in the past few years that social theory has been taken seriously within gerontology (Estes, Biggs, and Phillipson 2003).

Following comments by Bengston and colleagues (1997) on the lack of social theory in aging studies, the embryonic state of a sociological analysis of aging can be judged from the lack of refinement of the term "age." In Western societies, an individual's age is counted on a chronological foundation, beginning from birth to the current point of age, or when an individual has died. Counting age is a social construction because it is a practice underpinned by conceptions of time in regional, national, and global spaces (Powell 2001b), which came to be of increasing importance with the development of industrial capitalism (Phillipson 1982).

Furthermore, age has three main focal points of interest to its theorization. First, age and aging have a biological and physiological dimension, so that over time and space the appearances of physical bodies change (Longino and Powell 2004). Second, the aging of an individual takes place within a particular period of time and space. Third, as individuals, society has a number of culturally and socially defined expectations how people of certain ages are supposed to behave and how they are positioned and classified. "Old age," for instance, is difficult to define, especially for the state and its institutional branches. For example, for the United Kingdom's "Department of Pensions and Work," the legal concept of "pensionable age" has defined "old age" at sixty-five (Biggs 1999). The Department of Health's National Service Framework defines "old age" at fifty (Powell 2001c), yet the same U.K. department states that those people requiring intensive health services such as hospitals have been predominantly those older people aged seventy-five and over (Age Concern England 1997; Phillipson 1998). The British state is uncertain what old age can be defined as, but it is clear that biomedical models of aging and their viewpoints do influence societal perceptions of aging that impinge on social processes such as *life zones* of "health," "work" and "retirement" (Phillipson 1998).

It is particularly apt, then, to attempt to ground developments in a social theory that can be applied to questioning what we understand by "aging." It is also clear that theoretical perspectives need to be documented and analyzed in the light of the triumvirate of social, political, and economic transformations in Western society over the past fifty years. Indeed, the book also reflects on the modern/postmodern duality and how this continual provocative debate in social theory impinges on aging studies, by paying particular attention to examples drawn from biomedicine, social theory, popular culture, power relations, and risk.

MAPPING OUT THE TERRAIN: MODERN
AND POSTMODERN THEORIES OF AGING

What is a theory? A theory asks why a particular analogy is used to explain what is meant by aging and how the assumptions contained within biomedicine and policy spaces influence our understanding of the position of older people in contemporary society. Theories of aging are important in establishing frameworks for understanding, interpreting, and problematizing aging, how the processes of aging are contested and negotiated, and the interplay between various levels at which social relations take place—including hitherto neglected aspects of aging experience such as inequality, body and identity, technologies of power, and subjectivity and the risk society.

Ironically, the solutions to the "problems of aging" are tractable to disciplines such as gerontology, because they seem to promise answers to age prejudice and marginalization (Chudacoff 1989). For example, biomedical "solutions" address fears about mental and physical incapacity (Longino and Powell 2004). Medicine, with its focus on individual organic pathology and interventions, has also become a powerful and pervasive force in the definition and treatment of aging. The resulting "biomedicalization of aging" (Estes and Binney 1989) socially constructs old age as a process of decremental physical decline and places aging under the domain and control of biomedicine. It also encourages certain forms of the politics of aging: a focus on age as a question of social welfare, and a particular interpretation of the effects of risk and individualization. Theories of aging, albeit in contrasting ways, see these phenomena as indicating particular sites of resistance in which dominant biomedical conceptualizations of aging are to be contested and alternative explanations can be intimated.

For example, in stark contrast to the biomedical approach, the "political economy of old age" theoretical approach examines the structural inequalities that shape the everyday experience of growing old in modern society (Phillipson 1998).

THE ORGANIZATION OF THE BOOK

This book attempts to identify two central areas for the study of aging and the epistemological differences and continuities between them: *constructions of aging* (modern) and *deconstructions of aging* (postmodern). The book focuses on three general issues. One is the biomedical model and aging and its conceptual contestation. Another is the emergence of modernist social theories of aging, including the influence and dominance of three particular approaches: functionalist sociology and aging, political economy of old age and State power, and feminist approaches to aging. The book then attempts to move beyond these paradigms, with more of a focus on alternative and novel ways of theorizing aging through postmodernism and the aging body; Foucauldian approaches of power relations, surveillance and old age, risk, and aging identity; and, finally, "new horizons, old questions": rethinking social theory and aging.

Chapter 2 focuses on *modern constructions of aging*. The chapter identifies aging as a biomedically constructed concept. The medical dimension of aging and "the body" will be mapped out in relation to how old age has been categorized in modern society. The chapter allows the reader to understand how aging has been positioned by the dominant assumptions that underpin the "biomedical gaze" in contemporary society. The chapter locates biological and psychological models of aging and analyzes the prevalent discourses of aging that have helped to shape the perceptions of aging and the alleged limitations of such processes. The chapter also looks at counterexplanations of aging derived from social conceptual examinations, especially through the prism of social construction of aging (in particular, on demography as a social category).

Chapter 3 examines the postwar development of social theory and its relationship to the study of adult aging. Theoretical coverage of aging can be located to the early postwar years with Western government concern about the consequences of demographic change and the shortage of younger people in the U.S. and U.K. workforces (Phillipson 1998). In the postwar years, particular social theories surfaced which attempted to act in response to the social, health, and economic policy implications and projections of demographic change.

Alongside this, the chapter also traces the rise and consolidation of Functionalist "modernist" sociology that dominated the sociological landscape in the United States from the 1930s until the 1960s. The chapter analyzes the work of "disengagement theorists" of the structural-functionalist school regarding the study of aging and discusses the "political economy of old age" approaches of Carroll L. Estes (1979) and Minkler and Estes (1998). Similarly, in the United Kingdom, the writings of Alan Walker (1981), Peter Townsend (1981), and Chris Phillipson (1982, 1998) has added a critical sociological dimension to understanding age and aging, and it addresses the development of a feminist approach to adult aging and implications for theorizing aging. Finally, the chapter assesses the relevance of race and sexuality as key vehicles used to position the identities of older people but that have been overlooked by modernist theories of aging.

From chapter 4 on, the focus is on *deconstructions of aging*, moving beyond the earlier chapters by introducing new domains of theorizing aging. In particular, this chapter looks at incorporating "aging body" into postmodern dialogue. Henceforth, the chapter points to the emergence of cultural aspects of aging and the impact they have on postmodern understandings of the construction of the body and self-identity. Indeed, in modernist explanations of the aging body—that people's bodies develop from birth to childhood, to adulthood then on to old age—master narratives of "decay" and "deterioration" have been used to articulate the aging process and underlie the major claims made by the biomedical model.

However, according to Powell and Biggs (2004), the direct use of new technologies to either modify the appearance or performance of older people is symptomatic of postmodern times. To paraphrase Morris (1998), technologies here hold out the promise of "utopian bodies." Indeed, Haraway's (1991) novel reference to cyborgic interconnection of biological and machine entities has been influential to the emergence of postmodern gerontology. The chapter will examine postmodernism and its impact on social theory and its relevance to aging studies; understanding the aging body; cultural representations of aging; gender, culture, and aging; and biotechnology and aging process.

Chapter 5 reflects on what can be entitled "the Foucault Effect" on gerontological theorizing, with particular reference to aging and social welfare. Michel Foucault has devised concepts relevant to reconstructing an understanding of aging: "discourse," "power/knowledge," "technologies of self," and "governmentality." Whereas the Political Economy of Old Age school (cf. Phillipson 1998) and feminist gerontologists (Arber and Ginn 1995) look for the big picture of societal constructions of aging based on policy and resources, they miss one fundamental base: the "microphysics of power" and the relationship between professional experts and subjects/objects of power, in this case, older people (Foucault 1977).

Throughout his work, Foucault looked at the complex relationships between individuals at the microlevel and developed a concept of power. Indeed, we can explore what Foucault means by this by looking at power relations in every relationship: relations between teacher and pupil, doctor and patient, and social worker and client. The relevance to the social construction of aging is that its disciplinary knowledge base has been dominated by the figure of the "expert." Further, many biomedical researchers have perfected the technique of questionnaires to obtain the most intimate of personal information about "the elderly"; they profess their knowledge to be the "truth" because the methods they have used are scientific, and hence an expert is born:

> The judges of normality are everywhere. We are in the society of the teacher-judge, the doctor-judge, the educator-judge, the "social worker"-judge; it is on them that the universal reign of the normative is based; and each individual, wherever he may find himself, subjects to it his body, his gestures, his behaviour, his aptitudes, his achievements. The carceral network, in its compact or disseminated forms, with its systems of insertion, distribution, surveillance, observation, has been the greatest support, in modern society, of the normalizing power. (Foucault 1977, 304)

Clearly, this book distinctly separates Foucault's earlier structuralist work on discourse and later post-structuralist work on power/knowledge, governmentality and technologies of self from postmodernism in chapter 4. The movement of "postmodern gerontology" is seen mainly via work of Featherstone and Wernick (1995), who look at the fluidity of the aging body as a counter to modern classifications but do not make use of Foucault's work in their theorizing. In addition, the work of postmodern gerontology has centered on "positive aging," to which Foucault's work is not specifically bound, which, ironically, is more ontologically flexible in looking at power relations between professional experts and older people.

Chapter 6 looks at risk and individualization and their impingement on the aging process. Exploring the notion of *risk* puts forward two related arguments: first, that power relations, politics, world belief systems, and ageism, among other thing, shape our exposure, perception, and take-up of specific risks associated with aging; second, that these power relations also construct risk as a necessary and unavoidable discursive and material resource for identity formation. This can be seen in the shaping of aging as a form of risk.

Finally, chapter 7, the conclusion, focuses on *reconstructions of aging*. It suggests that broader insights from wider social theory are required to fully understand the processes and constructions of aging.

The book is not about biological or psychological aging, which is about how the body changes over time; rather, it is about the *discourses* and *processes* that impinge on *social construction* of aging through prisms of sociological theories. The emphasis is placed upon the processes of aging rather than aging itself.

It is anticipated that the epistemological and ontological debates discussed throughout the book will provoke thoughtful questions and potential explanations for the *social construction of aging* as it has been characterized in and by (post)modern society.

I

MODERN CONSTRUCTIONS OF AGING

an artificial language.

Occidental Modernity, the Biomedical Gaze, and Aging

INTRODUCTION

The focus on the science of "aging" is significant in the construction of powerful discourses of aging in modernity (Phillipson 1998; Powell and Biggs 2000). "Gerontology" itself is a broad discipline which encompasses psychological, biological, and social analyses of aging (Longino and Powell 2004). Since the beginning of the twentieth century, the biomedical study of aging, consisting of biological and psychological explanatory frameworks, has dominated the disciplinary development of gerontology (Katz 1996). Alongside this, Powell (2001b) has claimed that social theories of aging are relatively uncultivated territory. There has also been a small body of knowledge relating to social theories of social gerontology, which can be identified as: "Functionalist gerontology," which dominated post–World War II American sociology with activity and disengagement theories (Cumming and Henry 1961; Neugarten 1996); the development of structured dependency theory and "political economy of old age" gerontology in 1980s (Estes 1979; Estes and Associates 2001; Minkler and Estes 1998; Phillipson 1982, 1988, 1998); the growth of "feminist" gerontology in 1990s (Arber and Ginn 1995); and the evolution of "postmodern" gerontology toward the millennium (Gilleard and Higgs 2000; Longino and Powell 2004). As one can see, the social study of aging is a relatively new discipline of theoretical approaches, albeit with different interpretations of processes of aging.

17

Nevertheless, while these developments are growing in the construction of gerontological knowledge and are assessed in the next chapter, the biomedical model still eclipses the disciplinary dominance of gerontology (Biggs 1993; Phillipson 1998; Bengston, Burgess, and Parrot 1997; Moody 1998). An important point of clarification: while gerontology is defined as the study of the biological, psychological, and social aspects of aging, social gerontology is concerned especially with the impact of social and cultural conditions on the process of growing old. This chapter aims to understand the various changes that occur within the aging individual and how these factors influence perceptions and interactions within social environments. Social gerontology includes the study of societal attitudes toward aging and how these attitudes influence responses to the perceived needs of older persons, both on an interpersonal and structural level.

There are important implications here, not just for how aging is viewed by biomedical models of aging but for how society and its arrangement of political and economic structures create and sanction social policies grounded in such knowledge bases (cf. Powell 2001b). Such knowledge bases are focused on, (1) "biological aging," which refers to the internal and external physiological changes that occur in the individual body; and (2) psychological aging, understood as the developmental changes in mental functioning (i.e., emotional and cognitive capacities). Biomedical theories of aging can be distinguished from social constructions of aging by focusing (1) on the biopsychological constituent of aging; and (2) on how aging has been socially constructed. One perspective is driven from within and privileges the expression from inner to outer worlds. The other is much more concerned with the power of external structures that shape individuality. In essence, social constructionism poses the problem from the perspective of an observer looking in, while the biomedical model takes the position inside the individual, looking out (Biggs 1999).

Biomedical gerontology is a fundamental domain where medical discourses on aging have become located, and this is very powerful in articulating "truths" about aging (Estes and Binney 1989). Similarly, biomedical models of aging have also been prone to what Harry R. Moody (1998) refers to as an "amalgam of advocacy and science" in a neoliberal attempt to position individualized perceptions of aging. Under the guise of science and its perceived tenets of value-freedom, objectivity, and precision (Biggs 1993), biomedical gerontology has a cloak of legitimacy. However, a fundamental question is how biomedical gerontology has stabilized itself with a positivist discourse that not only reflects history but engages the total preoccupation of science and the "problems" of aging.

THE EMERGENCE OF BIOMEDICAL
SCIENCES OF AGING IN OCCIDENTAL MODERNITY

The biomedical model perceives of aging as a pathological problem tied to discourses of decline and dependency (Achenbaum 1978; Phillipson 1998). Thus, the "problem orientation" to aging is historically configured in the biomedical sciences and discourses that specialize in one terminology of gerontology (Powell and Biggs 2000). The medical science "problem" approach to aging can be related to how human subjectivity was structured as occidental modernity crystallized, when, beginning in the seventeenth and eighteenth centuries, the "social sciences," industrial capitalism, and bureaucratic politics simultaneously developed novel ways of objectifying individuals and populations in Western societies (Biggs and Powell 2001). The emergence of Western rationality was accompanied by a growth of scientific traditions such as positivism, each intellectualizing the nature and extent of individuality. Empirical observation, reason, and science are major themes of the modernist project. This is a set of beliefs about validating knowledge that has consolidated modernism. It arose from the intellectual diagnosis of society during and after the Enlightenment. It was the Age of Reason, in the second half of the eighteenth century—with the idea of progress elaborated by Immanuel Kant, Turgot, Condorcet—that gave rise to modernity (May 1996). The French Revolution in 1789—revolution based on reason—both expressed and gave momentum to this *new consciousness,* and the Industrial Revolution provided its material substance (Giddens 1991). This modern world, this new social order, was characterized by a new dynamism, a rejection of earlier traditions, a belief in progress, and the potential of human reason to promote freedom. Increasing rationality would enhance social understanding, order and control, justice, moral progress, and human happiness. Coupled with this was Rene Descartes's metaphysical axiom, "Cogito, ergo sum" (I think, therefore I am), which extolled the capacity of individual reason as the foundation of awareness and the locus of knowledge (May 1996). As a rationalist philosopher and mathematician, Descartes forcefully separated "mind" and "body" and thereby articulated a Cartesian dualism that has long provided a pivotal feature for the hegemony of Western culture.

Central to this Cartesian epistemology is a systematic belief in the supremacy of *logical reason over* the illogical nature, as such; Enlightenment philosophy assumes that the rational self has an "inner" relationship with the mind and an "outer" relationship with the body. Therefore, the body is conceived of as not a part of "who we are" but part of nature, hence an object to be controlled (Powell 2001e). With the Kantian philosophy of ethics, reason is identified with morality, for it provides the a priori principles for knowledge, certainty and universal law, whereas the body is identified with feelings and emotions, which are, according to Kant, external forms of determination; they imply a lack of freedom that takes individuals away from the path of pure reason (May 1996). Indeed, this very attitude of inflation toward the mind and deflation toward the body has long set the stage for transcendental ideals, in an attempt to articulate the order of the "empirical" world beyond its particularities and peculiarities and beyond its "immanence" (May 1996).

Indeed, the notion of transcendence went on to act as a basis for objective and universal knowledge, reinforcing the Cartesian "method" of existence and cognition and ratifying the need for disembodied experience, yet dialectically espousing a synthesis of mind and body in which the latter became the servant rather than the prison of the former. In fact, this disdain for the body entails a disdain for anything relating to it, such as emotions, feelings, and subjectivity. As such and in the episteme of transcendence, experience is deemed to be "real" only if deeply entrenched within consciousness and entirely detached from the corporeal. Personal subjectivity is thus regarded as a threat to the credibility and validity of experiential knowledge, and it can be transcended only if thawed into the crucible of "unity"—in other words, into the realm of Kant's unified "transcendental subjectivism" (May 1996). This transcendental idealism becomes the legacy of the androcentric, white, Christian, heterosexual culture (Powell and Longino 2001, 2002), in which reason and rationality are regarded as the source of the taken-for-granted superiority.

The causes and consequences of modernity are cultural, social, and metaphysical; but as Tim May (1996) points out, another driving force was capitalism, with its constant quest for new raw materials, new sources of labor power, new technologies, and new applications that might attract new consumers. From the outset, modernity promised to change the world in the name of Reason, and each innovation spawned another. However, alongside this, differentials, in terms of who may have access to and be able to deploy "reason," may also be seen to have served as a sophisticated legitimization function between scientific "experts" and the "subjects" of knowledge. For example, given the dichotomous relationship between repression and freedom, individuals will tend to define themselves via their position or identity within a power relationship, such as those of doctor to patient, judge to judged, or aged-care nurse to elderly patient.

Comparative research on aging in Eastern cultures has highlighted a path rather different from the conceptualization of aging as a scientific process developed by Western rationality. For example, Powell and Cook (2001) observe that traditional Chinese society placed older people on a pedestal. They were valued for their accumulated knowledge, their position within the extended family, and the sense of history and identity that they helped the family to develop (Powell and Cook, 2001). Respect for elderly people was an integral part of Confucian doctrine, especially for the family patriarch:

> The mixed love, fear and awe of the children for their father was strengthened by the great respect paid to age. An old man's loss of vigour was more than offset by his growth in wisdom. The patriarch possessed every sanction to enable him to dominate the family scene. (Fairbank 1959, in Powell and Cook, 2001, 55)

This was a view that was also prevalent in ancient Greece with the notions of respect for older people, especially regarding gendered issues of patriarchy (Bytheway 1995). Prior to industrialization, in India, it was understood that older people had responsible leadership roles and powerful decision-making positions because of their vast "experience," "wisdom," and "knowledge" (Katz 1996). It seems that, with the advent of Western science and rationality, aging began to be viewed in a context that was different from and more problematic than the Confucian doctrine of aging epitomized in China and traditions of respect for aging in India. Jacques Derrida (1978) makes the similar point when he spoke of the westernization of the world through the principles of Western science and language. Coupled with this, the idea of modernity evokes the development of capitalism and industrialization, as well as the establishment of nation-states and the growth of regional disparities in the world system. The period has witnessed a host of social and cultural transformations. Significantly, age categories emerged during this epoch as two fundamental axes along which people were exploited and societies stratified. A hallmark of modernity is the expansion of America and Europe and the establishment of Western cultural hegemony throughout the world. Nowhere is this more profound than in the production of scientific-technological knowledge about human behavior.

Indeed, the technological developments due to industrialization, westernization, and urbanization—under the purview of distorted forms of modernity—have neglected these statuses of aging by downgrading its conceptualization. Part of understanding individuality in Western culture, the birth of "science" gave legitimate credibility to a range of disciplines that were part of its umbrella. In particular, the biomedical model has become one of the most controversial yet powerful of both disciplines and practice with regard to aging (Powell and Longino 2002).

The biomedical model represents the contested terrain of decisions reflecting both normative claims and technological possibilities. Biomedicine refers to medical techniques that privilege a biological and psychological understanding of the human condition and rely upon scientific assumptions that position attitudes to aging in society for their existence and practice. As Arthur Frank (1991, 6) notes, the biomedical model occupies a privileged position in contemporary culture and society:

> Bio-Medicine [occupies] a paramount place among those institutions and practices by which the body is conceptualized, represented and responded to. At present our capacity to experience the body directly, or theorize it indirectly, is inextricably medicalized not sociologized.

The end product of this process in Western society is the biomedical model. Indeed, the mind-body dualism has become the location of regimen and control for emergence of the scientific in a positivist methodological search for objective "truth" (Longino and Powell 2004). By developing an all-encompassing range of biomedical discourses, many forms of social injustice, such as mandatory retirement and allocation of pensions, could be justified as "natural," inevitable, and necessary for the successful equilibrium of the social whole (Phillipson 1998).

The next section addresses the question as to how the biological body and psychological mind acquire meaning through the guise of science. If we focus on two models of gerontology, we can see the key assumptions that lie at the heart of biomedical definitional explanations of aging: biological and psychological dimensions. It must be stressed that biological and psychological gerontology has traditionally been articulated as the "biomedical model." While this is analytically useful, there is also a need to probe the similarities between biological and psychological aging and map out some of their main assumptions of human aging. Such a dual biological-psychology typology may have inclusions and omissions which may differ from other commentators but the broad aim is to provide a view of approaches to aging and the assumptions upon which they are based.

THE BIOMEDICAL MODEL:
BIOLOGICAL AND PSYCHOLOGICAL AGING

There has long been a tendency in matters of aging and old age to reduce the social experience of aging to its biological dimension from which are derived a set of normative stages, which overdetermine the experience of aging. Accordingly, being "old," for example, would primarily be a individualized experience of adaptation to inevitable physical and mental decline and of preparation for death (Biggs 1993). The paradox, of course, is that the homogenizing of the experience of old age compelled by such reliance on the biological dimension of old age is in fact one of the key elements of the dominant discourse on aging and old age.

Biological aging is a major facet of gerontology across and through U.S., European, and Western society as a whole (Katz 1996; Freund 1988). Before we assess the ramifications of biological aging and the way it colors particular discourses that have social implications for aging, it is important to contextualize its main assertions.

Biological approaches to aging have focused on searching for the reasons why and how human beings change over time in terms of physical and physiological characteristics. Bromley (1988, quoted in Hughes 1995, 29) suggests that aging is a degenerative process and contends that "aging can be conveniently defined as a complex, cumulative, time related process of biological and psychological deterioration occupying the post-development phase of life."

Furthermore, according to Biggs (1993) and Kunkel and Morgan (1999) the passage of time for human organisms is related to physical changes in and on the body: "hair loss" or "graying of hair," "decrease in reproductive system," and "cardiovascular functioning" are examples. These processes have been called "physiological changes" that are designed to contribute to the body's ability to function as it traverses the aging process.

Such bodily processes are designed to maintain a balance of internal working conditions called *homeostasis* (Kunkel and Morgan 1999). A key example of this scientific assumption is the relationship of oxygen to the blood system. Oxygen is transported by hemoglobin in the blood system to the body's 100 trillion cells (Kunkel and Morgan 1999). According to Timiras (1997), the inability of the body to maintain homeostasis compromises "normal functions" and "survival." The key issue here is one of internal body functions; however, there is another, wider question whether changes to the body exemplify "decline."

Kunkel and Morgan (1999) suggest that aging is often associated with a reduced ability to maintain homeostasis. According to Morris (1998), the potential of oxygen to all body cells decreases with age. However, changes outside the body, such as social factors or environmental pollution, may also disturb homeostasis (Phillipson 1998). However, the dominant narrative in the biological explanation of aging is that the ability to perform bodily functions will affect an individual's survival. The causal factors of the breakdown of these functions are essentially contested. Major causes of death at the turn of the twentieth century were infections and diseases, whereas major deaths in Western societies at the turn of the twenty-first century are chronic diseases: cardiovascular disease, cancer, and stroke (Powell 2001b). A posing question is whether these changes to the body are inevitable and natural consequences of aging. Aging, it seems, is linked with increased "risk" of illness and disease (Biggs 1993). The relationship is not necessarily causal: aging does not cause disease and disease does not cause aging.

According to Timiras (1997), biological aging affects every individual, evidencing itself overtly and covertly at different ages and in different organs and systems, depending on a whole series of cascading effects (Timiras 1997). Secondly, Timiras (1997) sees aging as a "deleterious" process, involving the functioning of cells and therefore organs and the organism itself.

We also know that age-related changes that do occur have a limiting effect on a number of bodily functions. Changes in the lens of the eye lead to presbyopia; changes in the cochlea of the ear lead to presbyacusis; a reduction in the accuracy of maintaining posture increases the amount of sway in the standing positions. (Timiras 1997, 55)

Another prominent example of biological gerontology is a focus on the pathological formation of "impairment in the body" (Bronley 1966, quoted in Hughes 1995, 25). It is partly assumed to be due to the aging process but it may be made worse by a "dementing process" such as Alzheimer's disease (Hughes 1995). According to Timiras (1997), "postural hypotension" is another of those problems that are age related. In age-related vulnerabilities, physiological systems decline with age, resulting in a shift in the competence of the body to control the chemical and cellular environment, thus leaving individuals more prone to so-called diseases of aging. In other words, the biological facet of aging is related to internal problems of the body as a person grows older. Coupled with this, there are certain biological viewpoints that suggest that older people have many "inevitable medical problems":

In fact, if one were to look at the presenting medical problems of the elderly, six symptoms would stand out: mental confusion, respiratory problems, incontinence, postural instability and falls, immobility and social breakdown. While they are problems of the elderly, no one has definitively shown robust evidence that they are age-related. It is mainly beyond the age of 75 and more particularly 85 years that frailty and the dependence associated with chronic illness becomes apparent. Yet, generally, these changes were going on for many years, at levels below which we are able to detect and associate conclusively with the age-related deterioration process. Conversations with medical personnel suggest that healthy elderly people quite often have laboratory test results which are slightly abnormal, but are not deemed significant. While there are many chance factors that may account for these "abnormalities," they may be precursors of cell or system age-related changes leading to expression of disease at a much later date. The sooner we identify signs of a disorder, the more likely treatment will be effective. (Timiras 1997, 54)

Despite the question of "inevitable" aging, in the United States the average life expectancy is approaching eighty years (Cook and Powell 2003); the fastest-growing segment of the U.S. population consists of persons aged eighty-five and over (Cook and Powell 2003). A key question for physiological theories is why bodies do not function eternally.

Biggs (1993) has suggested the following assumptions impinge on biological aging: that the human body is a machine, and overworked machines and human bodies "wear out" and "decline"; the human body grows but "decays" with time; "abnormal cells" are formed as a result or damage to DNA from "internal problems," all future cells are marked to be different, "in error" and "inferior" to the original intact parent cell; human skin "wrinkles" over time with passing of pigment cells; aging and death are built-in programmed events that result from genes "turning on" and "turning off" (for example, Timiras (1997) suggests there is gendered evidence for this among females such as menopause events; bodily aging causes problems of vision, hearing, and sensory function and balance. Healthy living and diet are seen as key shields to curtail the problems of biological aging (Gilleard and Higgs 2000). The individualized notion of aging as espoused by biological aging suggests that the body is in decline as an individual ages but declines especially sharply in "old age." The term *terminal decline* or *terminal drop* has been defined by Riegel and Riegel (1972, quoted in Kunkel and Morgan 1999, 33) as "a sudden drop in performance occurring within 5 years prior to death." As a phenomenon, terminal decline has been observed in the area of intellectual functioning in old age (Hughes 1995).

An interesting question is whether these physical changes are inevitable and "terminal" consequences of aging. The perceptions of aging through biology not only has postulated perspectives about aging but also there has been the psychological approach that has helped to coalesce particular discourses about aging.

Historically, the study of aging and old age was dominated by a Freudian paradigm that suggested that as individuals age and reach "old age" they are structured and regimented and not amenable to development or change. Psychology as a discipline of study had been much more concerned with childhood development (Hughes 1995). Like its biological counterparts, it saw the aging process as a decline in psychological well-being and adaptive ability as people enter old age. The framing of the psychological argument was that human functioning followed the biological journey of positive development in childhood, reaching a peak in early adulthood that was followed by inevitable decline, senescence, and loss of functions into old age.

Furthermore, according to Hughes (1995), psychological aging processes include changes in personality and mental functioning. According to Kunkel and Morgan (1999, 5): "changes are considered a 'normal' part of adult development, [and] some are the result of physiological changes in the way the brain functions."

However, there are psychologists such as Erik Erikson (1980) who see aging as development rather than as a degenerative process. Erikson (1980) hypothesized that each person's life progresses through a series of psychological stages, each of which is important in determining how an individual is able to meet the challenges of subsequent stages of life: infancy, childhood, adulthood, and old age.

This was also influential to the development of "successful aging" that has dominated psychological views of aging in recent years. Successful aging attempts a strategic understanding of late-life issues, grounded in psychological behavior that arises spontaneously among older people in particular (Baltes and Baltes 1990; Baltes and Carstersen 1996). It sidesteps the issue of prescribing contents by engaging with psychological processes, and thus moving from questioning the "what" of aging to the "how" (Baltes and Carstersen 1996).

This theoretical platform is based upon the observation that older people are in the main content with their lives, in spite of increasing "disability" or "hardship" (Hughes 1995). Baltes and Baltes (1990) suggest a "meta-model" of selective optimization with compensation to explain how older people negotiate both gains and losses that manifest with aging with such "psychological success." It is claimed that older people are satisfied because they have found personal and existential strategies to minimize the losses and maximize the gains encountered as individuals age. Nevertheless, as Baltes and Carstersen claim, we cannot predict any given individual's successful aging using this model unless "we know the domains of functioning and goals that the individual considers important, personally meaningful and in which he or she feels competent" (1996, 399).

According to Baltes and Carstersen (1996), this model has the advantage of acknowledging socioemotional dimensions of aging and multiple possibilities for self-development, and is based on the metapriority of mastering the challenges of aging, while allowing wide variety in the ways mastery can be achieved. Everyday existence is converted into successful activities, which are converted into life-satisfaction through techniques applied to the self. Harry R. Moody (1998) has quipped that the approach divides the population into the "wellderly" and the "illderly" and that Successful Aging is essentially about "surviving." Fundamentally, successful aging emerges as a normalizing identity approach, masking a decline model of aging. Ian Hacking (1990) claims that the notion of the "normal" identity provides a powerful framework for everyday life and individuals. As he states:

> The normal stands indifferently for what is typical, the unenthusiastic objective average but it also stands for what has been, good health, and for what shall be, our chosen destiny. That is why the benign and sterile sounding word "normal" has become one of the most powerful ideological tools of the twentieth century. (Hacking 1990, 23)

An analysis of successful aging reveals a distinctive and normalized category of aging has been created out of a psychologically defined "success." The category of aging and its coherence derives primarily from the exclusionary treatment on the basis of their psychological categorization and classification.

THE "DARK SIDE" OF BIOMEDICAL GAZE: THE CONSTRUCTION OF "PROBLEMS" OF AGING

> Old age is shamefully seen like head lice in children and venereal disease in their older siblings.
>
> —Stott 1981, 3

Biological and psychological characteristics associated with aging have been used to construct scientific representations of aging in modern society. The characteristics of biological aging as associated with loss of skin elasticity, wrinkled skin, hair loss, or physical frailty perpetuates powerful assumptions that help facilitate attitudes and perceptions of aging. It may be argued that rather than provide a scientific explanation of aging, such an approach homogenizes the experiences of aging by suggesting these characteristics are universal, natural, and inevitable. These assumptions are powerful in creating a knowledge base for health and social welfare professionals who work with older people in particular medical settings, such as a hospital or general surgery, and also for social workers (Powell and Biggs 2004). These new forms of social regulation were also reflected in the family and the community (Donzelot 1979; Delanty 1999). Hence, modern systems of social control have become increasingly bifurcated (Ignatieff 1978; Cohen 1985; Schrag 1980). Increasingly, modern society regulates the perception of the aging population by sanctioning the knowledge and practices of the new human sciences—particularly psychology and biology.

These are the gerontological "epistemes," "the total set of relations that unite at a given period, the discursive practices that give rise to epistemological figures, sciences and possibly formalised systems" (Foucault 1972, 191). The "psy" complex (or biomedical epistemes) refers to the network of ideas about the "nature" of individuals, their perfectability, the reasons for their behavior, and the way they may be classified, selected, and controlled (Howe 1994, 33–47). It aims to manage and improve individuals by the manipulation of their qualities and attributes and is dependent upon scientific knowledge and professional interventions and expertise. Human qualities are seen as measurable and calculable and thereby can be changed and improved. The new human sciences had as their central aim the prediction of future behavior (Ignatieff 1978). Indeed, the psy complex attempted to explain everything from one theory or viewpoint, that being via "infantile sexualism."

This speculative individualist reductionism was inadequate in explaining the complexities of various local group uprisings within society during the past hundred years. It was particularly weak in explaining the mentalities behind the masses of people who united as one individualized group to revolt gainst existing structures that had been suppressing both the individual's sense of "self" and the distinct groups with which they identified. For example, elderly people can be seen as such a distinct group labeled by the health assessments made of them to classify their existence into care by the state and by the care institutions that regulate and disseminate the authority to care staff to "manage" the elderly people (Powell and Biggs 2003).

Individuals who are subjected to multiple discourses are individuals with neuroses such as "dementia," "schizophrenia," or even "Alzheimer's disease" who are considered incapable of governing themselves and are subjected to the highest levels of control and surveillance.

Biggs (1993) suggests that a prevailing ideology of ageism manifests in the biomedical model by its suggestion that persons with such biological traits have entered a spiral of decay, decline, and deterioriation. Along with this goes certain assumptions about the ways in which people with outward signs of aging are likely to think and behave. For example, assumptions that "older people are poor drivers" or that older people have little interest in relationships that involve sexual pleasure are all explained away by the "decline" and "deterioration" master narratives that comprise a culture of aging. The effects of the decline-and-decay assumptions can be most clearly seen in the dominance of medico-technical solutions to the problems that aging and even an "aging population" (discussed below) (Phillipson 1998) is thought to pose. Here, the biomedical model has come both to colonize notions of age and to reinforce ageist social prejudices to the extent that "decline" has come to stand for the process of aging itself (Powell 1999).

The French social historian Michel Foucault has provided a shattering critique of medical sciences that can be used to assess the biomedical models of aging. Foucault (1967) was particularly interested in the limits and possibilities of discourses from "human sciences" (biology, for example) because of their attempts to define human subjectivity. Foucault (1977) shows the extent to which medicine objectifies the "sick" body, once it has been medicalized. For Foucault (1977) the body is thus not "natural" but "created" and reproduced through medical discourse. In *The Birth of the Clinic,* Foucault illustrates how the medical gaze opened "a domain of clear visibility" (1973, 105) for doctors, by allowing them to construct an account of the condition of the patient and to connect signs and symptoms with particular diseases. The space in which the gaze operated moved from the patient's home to the hospital. This, too, became the site for social work with older people, as well as the acquisition of knowledge; the object was the "elderly" body of the client. Similarly, the body of the "madman," according to Foucault, was viewed as "the visible and solid presence of his disease." Hence, the gaze focuses upon the body and "normalization" involved "treatment of the body" (Foucault 1967, 159–72).

Biomedicine became a disciplinary strategy that extended "control over minutiae of the conditions of life and conduct" (Cousins and Hussain 1984, 146) of individuals and understanding of bodies. Biomedical gerontology became an institution in its own right, in which the advice and expertise of biomedical professionals were geared to articulating "truths" about bodies (Armstrong, 1983). Medical domination through observation and scientific discourses objectified bodies appropriated through the aging process as "diagnoses began to be made of normality and abnormality and of the appropriate procedures to achieve the norm" (Smart 1985, 43). In this way examining the body and mind of older people was intrinsic to the development of power relationships in contemporary society: "The examination is at the center of the procedures that constitute the individual as effect and object of power, as effect and object of knowledge. It is the examination which by combining hierarchical surveillance and normalizing judgement, assures the great disciplinary functions of distribution and classification" (Smart 1985, 49).

The technique by which biomedicine has developed knowledge of aging is a slender aspect of disciplinary control and power (Katz 1996). This knowledge formation legitimizes the search within the individual body, for signs, for example, that he or she "requires" forms of surveillance and processes of medicalization (Powell and Biggs 2000). This legitimation permeates an intervention into older people's lives, because professional practices of surveillance are said to be appropriate for older people—because of the discourse of "declining" and pathological aging (Powell and Biggs 2000). Biomedicine, hence, constructs the identities of older people as objects of power and knowledge: "This form of power applies itself to immediate everyday life which categorises the individual, marks him by his own individuality, attaches him to his own identity, imposes a law of truth on him which he must recognise and which others have to recognise in him. It is a form of power which makes individuals subjects" (Foucault 1982, 212).

Thus Foucault (1973) has argued persuasively that the birth of the medical profession brought with it a different way of seeing illness and well-being related to structural and personal spaces. Most notably, the older people who became sick became an object to be modified (Powell and Biggs 2000). Under the "biomedical gaze," people become their bodies, bodies disaggregated into a series of dysfunctional parts. This is useful for the biomedical scientific analysis of function and remedy but severely limits any perspective that takes into account interpersonal and wider social factors.

The dominance of the biomedical model has engendered negative conceptualizations pertaining to aging. It has also sought to reinvent itself as the "savior" of the aging via the biotechnological advancements that foster reconstruction of the body and to prevent the aging process (Wahidin and Powell 2001; Powell and Biggs 2004). It appears that:

> established and emerging master narratives of biological decline on the one hand and consumer agelessness on the other co-exist, talking to different populations and promoting contradictory, yet interrelated, narratives by which to age. They are contradictory in their relation to notions of autonomy, independence and dependency on others, yet linked through the importance of techniques for maintenance, either via medicalised bodily control or through the adoption of "golden-age" lifestyles. (Biggs and Powell 2001, 97)

Biomedical gerontology has attempted to legitimize its existence by playing "games of truth" (Foucault 1980), claiming aging is a "universal" problem but, on other hand, aging could be "cured" by biomedical intervention for potential "aging consumers" (Biggs and Powell 2001; Powell 2001b; Gilleard and Higgs 2000). Such intervention could include swapping organs from one body to the next; by paying for expensive forms of surgery and modification: plastic surgery; hip replacements; cyborgic facilitation of bodily parts and functions. Indeed, the anti-aging industry has boomed in recent years with regard to such reconstruction, but the boom is premised on consumerism. Science itself has suggested that secrets of eternal youth can be found in genetic codes and that using stem-cell research could curtail the aging process. Aging becomes governed by regiments of exercise in which individuals become the object of their own gaze in order to maintain their commitment to achieving a particular body project generated through discourses from science. Biomedicine may make people "healthier" and "live longer," but they are still not freer from the structures imposed upon them within their society. Biomedicine may allow older people to live longer and may be even empower them with new technologies and interventions and an awareness of how to encourage healthy aging (Gilleard and Higgs 2000). However, biomedicine still struggles with the notion that being old is positive, in relation to the ideology of aging, especially old age as "decrepit," from decades of negatively stereotyping senescence. These structures change within biomedicine in order to reconstruct narratives of aging, but their dominant discourse of decline is still their master narrative of legitimacy. In order for individuals to survive within contemporary society, the argument espoused is that they must change their attitudes to enjoy the "benefits" of healthy aging professed by biomedical expert powers; aging needs modification as though it were a medical problem to begin with.

Research by Powell and Biggs (2000) indicates that medical discourses of power play a key interventionist role in societal relations and in the management of social arrangements. That is, medical "experts" pursue a daunting power to classify, which has serious consequences for the reproduction of knowledge. The power to classify also serves to maintain power relations (Powell and Biggs 2000). Likewise, we must "challenge the hermeneutic belief in deep meaning by tracing the emergence of sexual confession and relating it to practices of social domination" (Dreyfus and Rabinow 1983, xxv). The significance of biomedical practices reveals an interesting transition in attitude and inward approach to the psyche in both the personal and professional realm of care for older people. The "subject" of biomedicine becomes an "object" when these "speaking subjects" proliferate discourses or narratives that can be analyzed once again for the power relations embedded in their language. As Dreyfus and Rabinow (1983, xxv) assert, this demonstrates that "deep meaning is a cultural construction" accessible by analysis of the culturally constructed language used by subjects. The individual once again is not a free or liberated individual, but one who is culturally regulated by the social order and under surveillance by biomedical powers that can repress individuals with their diagnostic classifications.

Following Powell and Biggs (2000) a dense form of biomedical discourses, containing alleged universal truths, totalizing views, and master narratives with which to explain and understand almost every aspect of social life, play a central role in the construction of physical and symbolic boundaries, and it is through them that both expert groups and individuals come to know and understand the social world and constitute their social identities. As part of this process, certain powerful voices, such as those of geriatricians, increase their legitimacy, while other, often dissenting, voices of older people become delegitimized (Biggs and Powell 2001).

Embedded is a relationship of power in that the classifier or medical expert doing the diagnosing would have the upper hand over the person being classified or diagnosed. The diagnostic knowledge they possessed placed them in an empowered position of authority, affirmed by their expert titles, to exert claims over their patients and police their welfare.

AGING: A SOCIAL CONTEXT

Estes and Binney (1989) have used the expression "biomedicalization of aging," which has two closely related narratives: (1) the *social construction of aging* as a medical problem; (2) *ageist practices and policies growing out of thinking of aging* as a medical problem. They suggest:

> Equating old age with illness has encouraged society to think about aging as pathological or abnormal. The undesirability of conditions labeled as sickness or illness transfer to those who have these conditions, shaping the attitudes of the persons themselves and those of others towards them. Sick role expectations may result in such behaviors as social withdrawal, reduction in activity, increased dependency and the loss of effectiveness and personal control—all of which may result in the social control of the elderly through medical definition, management and treatment. (Estes and Binney 1989, 588)

Estes and Binney (1989) highlight how individual lives and physical and mental capacities which were thought to be determined solely by biological and psychological factors are, in fact, heavily influenced by *social environments* in which people live. This remains invisible to the biomedical approach because these biological and psychological factors stem from the societal interaction before becoming embedded and recognizable as an "illness" in the aging body of the person. For example, in the "sociology of emotions," the excursion of inquiry has proposed that "stress" is not only rooted in individualistic emotional responses but also regulated, classified, and shaped by social norms of Western culture (Powell and Biggs 2003). This type of research enables the scope of aging to be broadened beyond biomedical individualistic accounts of the body. On this basis alone, sociology has invited us to recognize that aging is not merely a socially constructed problem, as viewed by biomedical sciences, but is also the symptomatic deep manifestation of underlying relations of power and inequality that cuts across and through age, class, gender, disability, and sexuality (Powell and Biggs 2000; Powell 2002). At this level of analysis, sociology addresses biomedicine as one of the elements of social control and domination legitimated through power/knowledge of "experts" (Foucault 1972, 1982; Biggs and Powell 2000; Powell and Biggs 2000; Powell and Biggs 2004). Such expert formation has also been labeled as ageist (Bytheway 1995). Ageism is defined as negative assumptions made about old age that treat older people not as individuals but as a homogenous group that can be discriminated against on the basis of their age (Bytheway 1995).

Every society uses age categories to divide this ongoing process into stages or segments of life. These life stages are socially constructed rather than inevitable. Aging, too, is a production of social categorizing. At any point in the life span, age simultaneously denotes a set of social constructs, defined by the norms specific to a given society at a specific point in history. Thus, a specific period of life—infancy, childhood, adolescence, adulthood, middle age, or old age—is influenced by the structural entities of a given society. Therefore, aging is not to be considered the mere product of biological-psychological function but, rather, a consequence of sociocultural factors and subsequent life-chances.

Modern society has a number of culturally and socially defined notions of what Thomas R. Cole and associates (1992) calls the "stages of life." Historically, the stages of life were presented as a religious discourse that formed the basis for the cultural expectations about behavior and appearance across the life-course into old age. As Andrew Achenbaum (1978, 2) perceptively claims: "[P]eople at the end of the life-cycle continuum have constantly been described as 'old.' Old age is an age-old phenomenon."

Indeed, the life-stage model, still used in taken-for-granted popular usage in our society, influences how our lives are structured, albeit by means of biomedical discourses of "decline" (Jefferys and Thane 1989). As Thomas (1977, quoted in Powell and Biggs 2000, 17) points out succinctly: "Of all divisions in human society, those based on age appear the most natural and the least subject to historical change. The cycle of infancy, youth, maturity and decline seems an inexorable process."

In Occidental societies, an individual's "age" is counted on a chronological or numerical foundation, beginning from birth to the current point of age, or when an individual has died. Chronological aging is a habit individuals engage in: "birthdays" and "wedding anniversaries," for example. Counting age can be seen as a social construction because it is a practice underpinned by the development of industrial capitalism (Phillipson 1998). Hence, what is critical about aging, then, is how a society uses it to socially construct people into "categories." As a classificatory tool, age is important in three ways. First, like sex, age is an *ascribed* status or characteristic, based on attributes over which we have little or no control. Second, unlike sex, a specific age is always transitional—constantly moving from one age to another, beginning life at zero and ending with a certain number at death. These transitions also assume that conformity is rewarded whereas deviance is punished; they are regulated by societal expectations of age-appropriate behavior. Third, although in every society some age groups are more powerful, rich, and respectable than others, the unique aspect of aging is that everyone can expect to occupy various positions throughout life on the basis of his or her age. Coupled with this, ideas that centered on social aging coalesced as a theoretical orientation on aging during the 1960s and 1970s. In 1974, Bernice L. Neugarten wrote an influential essay marking a distinction between what is now referred to as the third and fourth ages, the early years of retirement and the later ones. Neugarten (1974) referred to persons in these stages of later adult development as the "young-old" and the "old-old." The young-old are like late-middle-aged persons. They generally have good health and they are about as active as they want to be. The old-old, however, tend to be widowed and are much more likely to be living dependently. Consequently, the concept of old age, with its attending miseries, was only pushed later into the life-course by this reconceptualization. The first decade after the beginning of Social Security retirement benefits seem like "the second middle age," but the biomedically framed "declining body" remains an issue in the fourth, old-old age (Longino and Powell 2004).

THE DEMOGRAPHIC CONSTRUCTION OF AGING: COMPARING THE UNITED STATES, THE UNITED KINGDOM, AND CHINA

Since the turn of the last century, the life expectancy of people born in the United States has increased by approximately twenty-five years and the proportion of persons sixty-five years or older has increased from 4 percent to over 13 percent. By the year 2030, one in five individuals in the United States is expected to be sixty-five years or older and people age eighty-five and older make up the fastest-growing segment of the population. In 2000, there were thirty-four million people aged sixty-five or older in the United States who represented 13 percent of the overall population. By 2030 there will be seventy million over sixty-five in the United States, more than twice their number in 2000. Distinguished scholar and president of the Gerontological Society of America Charles F. Longino (1994) believes that, thanks to better health, changing living arrangements, and improved assistive devices, the future may not be as negative as we think when we consider an aging population. Thirty-one million people, or 12 percent of the total population, are aged sixty-five and older. In another thirty-five years, the aging population should double again. The aging population is not only growing rapidly, but it is also getting older: "In 1990, fewer than one in ten elderly persons was age 85 or older. By 2045, the oldest old will be one in five. Increasing longevity and the steady movement of baby boomers into the oldest age group will drive this trend" (Longino 1994, 856).

Comparatively, the population structure of western European countries including the United Kingdom has changed since the turn of the twentieth century. Whereas in 1901, just over 6 percent of the population were at or over current pension age (sixty-five in the U.K. for men and women), this figure rose steadily to reach 18 percent in 2001 (Powell 2001b). At the same time, the population of younger people under age sixteen fell from 35 percent to 20 percent. The United Nations estimates that by the year 2025, the global population of those over sixty years will double, from 542 million in 1995 to around 1.2 billion people (Krug 2002, 125).

Alan Walker (1985) argues that the demographic situation for "the population aged 65 and over is set to increase steadily (by one fifth overall) between 1983 and 2021. However the largest rises are due to the numbers aged 75 and over and 85 and over: 30 percent and 98 percent respectively. By the end of this period women will outnumber men in the 85 and over age group by around 2.5 to 1" (Walker 1985, 4).

Thus, the age structure of the population has changed from one in which younger people predominated to a society in which people in later life constituted a substantial proportion of the total population. While the biological and psychological models of aging describe it as an "inevitable" and "universal" process, such terms cannot apply to the aging of an entire aging population. Transformations in the age profile of a population are a response to political and economic structures.

This has been coined as an "aging population" by governments of left and right persuasion and indicative of Eastern and Western cultures. Earlier, we examined the biomedical model and its theoretical assumptions of "decline." Not only has the aging process been viewed as a medical problem but it has also been viewed as a social problem: a "burden" population group. As we discussed earlier, the central focus of modern social systems of regulation is the classification of the "aging population" based on the scientific claims of different experts in the "psy" complex (Biggs and Powell 2001).

Older people in particular constitute a large section of populations in Western society, but the percentage of pensionable age is projected to remain at 18 percent until 2011, when it becomes 20 percent, and to rise to 24 percent in 2025 (Phillipson 1998). In relation to public services that have to be paid for by younger working people, the burden is expressed in alarming percentages. Nor are only older people seen as dependent; children under school-leaving age and people over the retirement age are similarly classified. Dependency rates, that is, the number of dependents relative to those of working age, have altered little over the twentieth century, and yet the notion of a "burden" group retains its currency. The reason for its persistence is that during a period of rapid growth of aging populations there has been a fall in the total fertility rate (the average number of children that would be born to each woman if the current age-specific birthrates persisted throughout her childbearing life

Changes in the age structures of societies also affect total levels of labor force participation in society, because the likelihood that an individual will be in the labor force varies systematically by age (Walker 1985; Phillipson 1998). Concurrently, global population aging is projected to lead to lower proportions of the population in the labor force in highly industrialized nations, threatening both productivity and the ability to support an aging population (Krug 2002).

Meanwhile, the young adult population in Third World countries has been growing rapidly. The World Bank foresees growing threats to international stability as different demographic-economic regions are pitted against one another. The United Nations recognizes important policy challenges, including the need to reverse recent trends toward decreasing labor force participation of workers in late middle and old age, despite mandatory retirement in certain Western countries such as the U.K. (Powell 2001c). Social welfare provisions and private-sector pension policies influencing retirement income have a major impact on retirement timing.

Hence, a major concern for organization such as the United Nations and World Bank centers on the number of such "dependent" older people. Using evidence from the U.K., the percentage of people of working age, that is, sixteen to sixty-four, will drop from 64 percent in 1994 to 58 percent in 2031 (Powell 2001c). As the number of workers per pensioner decreases, there will be pressure on pension provision. This is evident now, in such areas as pensions and long-term care; the retreat of the state made evident in the erosion of State Earnings Related Pay (SERPS) is forcing people to devise their own strategies for economic survival in old age (Alcock 1996). In the British context that also impinges on Western societies in general, private pensions are slowly being introduced in order to prevent the "burden" of an aging population. These are ways in which the state continues to use "apocalyptic projections" such as a "demographic time bomb" about aging populations in order to justify cuts in public expenditure (Warnes 1996). The British newspaper **the** *Guardian* has echoed such fears of a moral panic of old age by stating:

> A demographic time bomb to tick into the next century—This year, Britain will be attempting to grapple with the implications of the . . . time bomb—the decline of the British teenager, and the rise . . . in the proportion of old people in the community. (*Guardian*, 2 January 1989, 17).

This type of "moral panic" (cf. Cohen 1985) has knock on effects and reflects profoundly rooted ambivalence toward older people that can lead to an exaggeration of the size of resources required to meet their needs or of the sacrifice required by the sixteen-to-sixty-four age group via taxation (Harper and Laws 1995). Hence, it is not simply that governments and researchers have belatedly recognized "the greying" of populational constructions and policy implications; it is that they continue to look for knowledge of aging as the power to define old age as a social problem. An aging population, like that of an individual being studied by biomedical models, is seen as a "burden" problem in terms of economic management of Western economies. Is this the case with Eastern societies?

Comparatively with China, Du and Tu (2000) identify four "unique characteristics" of China's aging population:

1. *Unprecedented speed:* The proportion of aging population is growing faster than that of Japan, the country previously recognized as having the fastest rate, and much faster than nations in Western Europe, for example.

2. *Early arrival of an aging population:* Before modernization has fully taken place, with its welfare implications. "It is certain that China will face a severely aged population before it has sufficient time and resources to establish an adequate social security and service system for the elderly" (Du and Tu 2000, 79).

3. *Fluctuations in the total dependency ratio:* The Chinese government estimates are that the country will reach a higher "dependent burden" earlier in the twenty-first century than was previously forecast.

4. *Strong influence of the government's fertility policy and its implementation on the aging process:* The SCFP means fewer children being born, but with more elderly people a conflict arises between the objectives of limiting population increase and maintaining a balanced age structure.

The combination of such factors means that the increased aging population is giving rise to serious concerns among Chinese policy makers. Age embraced by "respect" in Confucian doctrine has been reconstructed through governmental populational discourses of "risk," "danger," and "threat."

It could be argued, when looking at the effects of a so-called demographic time bomb across the United States, Europe, and Asia, that it may have been grossly exaggerated (Powell and Cook 2001). Such a negative perception of old age has developed via a process of ageism—stereotyping older people simply because of their chronological age. Ageist stereotypes such as "aging populations" act to stigmatize and consequently marginalize older people and differentiate them from groups across the life-course who are not labeled "old" (Bytheway 1995).

One of the ways to interpret social aging, whether it be in individual or populational terms, is by theorizing about what it means to age in a society; that is, what concerns and social issues are associated with aging and how these themes are influenced by, and at the same time influence, the society in which people live. Thus, to understand the process of aging, looking through the lens of the "sociological imagination" (Mills 1959) is not to see it as an individualized problem but, rather, as a societal issue that is faced by both the developed and underdeveloped nations as a whole.

We do need to ask, How has age been theorized by social theories of gerontology? Different sociological theories of old age are concerned with the social significance of age. Some are concerned with the individual's adjustment to growing older and others are concerned with the relative distribution of the material disadvantage of older people. There is a somewhat heterogeneous bundle of theoretical disciplines, each with a differentiation of concerns, strengths, and weaknesses. Modernist social theories in social gerontology have been the major explanations of what forms of social activity take place in Western society and in a given historical time. Such modernist theories have shaped perceptions about aging and the nature of the relationship of the individual to modern society related to function, conflict, and gender. The next chapter focuses on these concerns.

3

Theorizing Aging

Critical Explorations of Modernist Sociological Approaches

INTRODUCTION: AGING AS SOCIALLY CONSTITUTED

The previous chapter highlighted the power of the biomedical gaze regarding the positioning of aging as a problem-based discourse in modernity. There has long been a propensity in matters of aging and old age to engage in the ontological and epistemic reductionism of aging to its biological and psychological dimensions. Indeed, in Western culture, aging came to be understood in terms of biological science to be only material, and the scientific approach to medicine became overwhelmingly objective, reductionistic, and rational. These scientific dimensions primarily are a set of normative "stages" of body and mind process that position the experiences and representations of aging and old age in Western culture (Gilleard and Higgs 2000). As the preceding chapter indicated, for the biomedical model, growing old would primarily be a process of inevitable physical and mental "decline" and of preparation for the ultimate ending: death itself. The paradox, of course, is that the biomedical homogenizing of the experience of old age which the reliance on the biological and psychological dimensions of aging entails is in fact one of the key elements of the (public) dominant "commonsense" discourses on aging and old age. A deeper understanding of aging requires, however, that we move beyond commonsense approaches and broaden our view to understand how processes, from the biomedical level of the individual cell to overall society, influence us, and in turn are influenced by us as individuals progressing through the life-course.

We also highlighted how aging was a social category in terms of social constructionism with reference to its definition as both a categorization and populational construct. The biomedical and social conceptualizations of aging demand theoretical interrogation of what Phillipson (1998) calls the "social construction of aging." The social construction of aging is an important process in debunking discourses of "truth" and can be used as an alternative to narrow medical narratives (Powell 2002); it includes how "norms" or pervasive attitudes materialize—from basic biomedical functions to sophisticated and complex social/cultural structures including educational, political, and religious institutions, the arts, customs, morality, ethics, and law.

Social constructs are enormously powerful in determining individual and collective identity because they answer profound existential questions: Who am I? Where do I belong? What do I do? How do I do it? Where am I? Why am I? Who are you? Why are you? Those in power present ontologically arbitrary social constructs as "the way life actually is," that is, as reality. For example, biomedical sciences have been important in this process in shaping reality regarding the aging process. The social constructions of aging assert that aging has no existence independent of social interaction and power relationships in society; they are not grounded in "nature" as is biomedical gerontology under the auspices of biological-psychological gerontological knowledge (the meaning of which is itself socially determined). Indeed, the constructedness of aging is made invisible by the normal workings of social life, so that it appears natural rather than artificial. Social constructionism is therefore about helping individuals to stand outside their own prejudices and see the notion of the "other" in order to explain and understand what may be happening in the social world, given that reality is increasingly seen as fragile, shifting, and coexisting with different "realities." Further, embracing the social construction of aging can help individuals blame themselves less for their "problems" and strive to change limiting biomedical discourses of human behavior.

The promise of a sociology of aging then could transcend narrow biomedical explanations; it might take a cue from C. Wright Mills's tour de force *The Sociological Imagination* (1959). Mills suggested that the promise and responsibility of the discipline of sociology lie in giving individuals the conceptual tools to make distinctions between "personal troubles" and "public issues." Social theorists can make this distinction if they have a social context and a sense of history from which to understand personal experiences.

The ability to shift perspectives, to analyze an experience or an issue from many levels of analysis and to see the intersection of these levels and mutual influence, is the heart of the sociological imagination. If we develop a new understanding of our own attitudes about aging because we learn about how societies construct meanings of age, then we will have experienced the "sociological imagination." As Mills (1959, 5) points out: "No social study that does not come back to the problem of biography, of history and of their intersections within a society has completed its intellectual journey."

Mills suggests that there are three fundamental questions we must ask in exercising our "sociological imagination":

a) What is the structure of this particular society as a whole?; b) Where does this society stand in human history? What are the essential features of this period?; c) What "varieties" of people prevail in this society and in this historical period? How are these types "selected and formed, liberated and repressed"?

With these "tools for thinking," Mills focuses our attention on the broad social structures that shape our personal stories. Equipped with this understanding, we can go on to understand how "by the fact of our living, we contribute, however minutely, to the shaping of our society and the course of history, even as we are made by society and its historical push" (Mills 1959, 4). In order to understand aging we need to be aware of how our personal knowledge is shaped by ourselves and by society as a whole.

Drawing from this definition and process of the "sociological imagination" and the interplay between social context and individuals; the sociology of aging can be defined as the systematic study of the taken-for-granted assumptions that are socially constructed by society and filter through to shape personal attitudes about aging in everyday life. The sociology of aging is also the study of the relationships between institutions and individuals in society. The sociology of aging provides an analytical framework for understanding the interplay between human lives and changing social structures. Sociologists are interested, therefore, in how society works, the arrangements of its structure and institutions, and the mechanisms of its processes of change.

Hence, the sociology of aging is important in examining the interdependence between aging over the life-course as a social process and societies and groups as classified by age. The field of social gerontology contributes to it through reformulation of traditional emphases on process and change and on the multidimensionality of sociological concerns as they touch on related aspects of other social science disciplines.

The field of social gerontology is concerned with both basic sociological research on age and its implications for social theory as well as policy and professional practice. Nevertheless—and it is almost an embarrassing statement to make—as a field of study, mainstream sociology has not been interested in the sociology of aging. As Powell (2002) point outs, in male-dominated sociology the study of aging has been seen as one of the lowest-status areas of all. Despite the poverty of theory in social gerontology in recent years (Bengston, Burgess, and Parrot 1997), this chapter interrogates and problematizes the ways social theories have arisen in relation to interpretations of aging, with particular focus to American and British social gerontology.

This chapter focuses on highlighting the major theoretical schools in social gerontology by addressing functionalist gerontology, political economy of old age, and feminist gerontology. It is arguable that these three theoretical models of aging are dominant in modernist constructions of knowledge of aging, but they remain important reference points about the nature of aging and its structural, interpersonal, and esoteric constructions. The chapter then introduces two essential identity variables that have been historically omitted as to fully understanding the complexity of aging in modernity: race and sexuality.

THE GAZE OF FUNCTIONALIST GERONTOLOGY

In the postwar years, social gerontology emerged as a multidisciplinary field of study that attempted to respond to the social, health, and economic policy implications and projections of populational change in Western society (Phillipson 1998). The disciplinary subject matter of social gerontology encompassed a wide range of social science approaches (economic, political science, and human geography, as well as sociology) that was shaped by significant external forces: first, by state intervention to achieve specific outcomes in health and social policy for older people; secondly, by a sociopolitical and economic setting that viewed an aging population as creating a "social problem" for Western society in general (Phillipson 1998).

However, it was not until the 1950s that social analysis of aging began to emerge in its own right. In the United States, it is significant that this growth was underpinned by the involvement and interest of notable functionalist sociologists who helped lay the foundations for the rapid growth of the discipline between the 1950s and 1975.

In postwar Great Britain, by contrast, social research on old age was largely subsumed within the wider concerns of the expanding welfare state, and it has only recently emerged as a field of academic study in its own right. Considerable shifts in socioeconomic policy and demographic changes have set the stage for what is an increasingly important debate on the interpretation of aging. Until the 1990s, not only was age subsumed under race, class, and gender, but the dominant explanatory framework concerning aging came, as we discussed earlier, from outside of sociology: the so-called medical model. So it is of central importance that aging came to be looked at in social terms.

The important point to note is that theories often mirror the norms and values of their creators and their social times, reflecting culturally dominant views of what should be the appropriate way to analyze social phenomena (Kalish 1979; Turner 1989). The two functionalist theories that dominated U.S. gerontology in the 1950s and 1960s, the disengagement and activity theories, follow this normative pattern. Both disengagement and activity theories not only postulate how individual behavior changes with aging, but also imply how it should change.

Disengagement Theory

Functionalist sociology dominated the sociological landscape in the United States from the 1930s until the 1960s (Blaikie 1999). In the 1940s, functionalist gerontologists were already obsessed with the consequences of role loss among older people. Old age, characterized as a "roleless role" (Cumming and Henry 1961) was seen as a period of life in which feelings of dissatisfaction and low morale prevailed. However, as Dowd points out, the antidote to these "miseries" became part of standard gerontological wisdom by the early 1950s: remain active and make creative uses of leisure time. To this way of thinking, meaning is imposed from the outside and resides primarily in societal tasks and duties such as work and childrearing. Except for some concern for the socially isolating aspects of physical frailty, the body was not a major concern of these scholars.

This view of aging appeared in the United States in the dominant structural-functionalist school via the work of "disengagement theorists" (Phillipson 1998). Such major protagonists of disengagement theory were Cumming and Henry (1961), who looked at how older people should disengage from work roles and prepare for the ultimate disengagement: death (Powell 2000, 2001a). They also proposed that gradual withdrawal of older people from work roles and social relationships is both an "inevitable" and "natural" process: "withdrawal may be accompanied from the outset by an increased preoccupation with himself: certain institutions may make it easy for him" (Cumming and Henry 1961, 14).

Cumming and Henry (1961) maintained that the process of disengagement—an inevitable, rewarding, and universal process of mutual withdrawal of the individual and society from each other with advancing age—was normal and to be expected. This theory argued that it was beneficial for both the aging individual and society that such disengagement take place in order to minimize the social disruption caused by an aging person's eventual death (Neugarten, 1996). Cumming and Henry's disengagement theory of aging proclaims that the aged individuals must be deposed from their various roles for the proper functioning of the society. According to the proponents of this theory, disengagement is a gradual and an inevitable process. Moreover, disengagement theory confines the area of operation of the aged by restricting their scope for employment and commitments. In essence, though controversial, the theory is normative in claiming that disengagement of older people is functional— it offers psychological well-being to older individuals (Cumming and Henry 1961).

Retirement is an example of the disengagement process, enabling older persons to be freed of the roles of an occupation and to pursue other roles not necessarily aligned with generating income. Through disengagement, Cumming and Henry (1961) argued, society anticipated the loss of aging people through death and brought "new blood" into full participation within the social world.

Bronley (1966, quoted in Bond and Coleman 1993, 43) further asserts that "in old age, the individual is normally disengaged from the main streams of economic and community activity."

Not surprisingly for Bromley (1966, quoted in Bond and Coleman 1993, 44): "The (disengagement) process is graded to suit the declining biological and psychological capacities of the individual and the needs of society."

In order to legitimize its macrogeneralizations, disengagement theory boasted of the objective and value-free rigor of its research, citing its survey and questionnaire methods of gerontological inquiry. In a sense, arguing for disengagement from work roles under the guise of objectivity, based on scientific method, gives governments a very powerful argument for legitimizing the definitions of who can work and who cannot, based on age (Powell 1999).

Activity Theory

The second functionalist theory, activity theory, is a counterpoint to disengagement theory, since it claims that a successful old age can be achieved only by maintaining roles and relationships (Powell 2001). Activity theory actually predates disengagement theory. In the 1950s Havighurst and Albrecht (1953, cited in Katz 1996) insisted aging can be a lively and creative experience. For activity theorists, disengagement is not a natural process, as advocated by Cumming and Henry. For activity theorists, disengagement theory is inherently ageist and does not promote, in any shape or form, "positive ageing" (Estes, Biggs, and Phillipson 2003).

The activity theory of aging, developed by Havighurst, B. Neugarten and Tobin (Powell 2000), has developed a different approach for the elderly in modern society. According to Powell (2001c), this theory is regarded as an anti-aging perspective and maintains that, if the roles and activities associated with old age are lost, it is important to develop a new set of roles and activities in order to replace them. Thus, replacement of roles and activities is compulsory for the aged because it enhances their life satisfaction. In fact, the activity theory can best be attributed to the perspective of emancipation.

The point here is that old age was understood to be a uniform process and a uniformly problematic and depressing state. Older persons' only hope for contentment lay in increasing their level of social activity.

Nevertheless, activity theory neglects issues of power, inequality, and conflict between age groups. An apparent "value consensus" may reflect the interests of powerful and dominant groups within society who find it advantageous to have age/power relations organized in such a way. While Phillipson (1998) sees such functionalist schools as important in shaping social theory responses to them, such functionalist theories impose a sense of causality on aging by implying that one will either "disengage" or will be "active" in old age. Such theories of aging are very macro-oriented and fail to resolve tensions within age-group relations that impinge upon the interconnection of race, class, and gender with age (Powell 1999).

POLITICAL ECONOMY OF OLD AGE
AND THE POLITICS OF DISTRIBUTION

"Political economy of old age" was coined (cf. Estes 1979) as a critical response to theoretical dominance of functionalism and the epistemic normative explanatory frameworks: either disengage or be active. Political economy of old age emerged as a critical orthodoxy that focused on how the state and its resources and institutions positioned the experiences and life-chances of older people in capitalist Western society (Phillipson 1998).

Arguably, this critical branch of political economic gerontology grew as a direct response to the hegemonic dominance not only of structural functionalism, in the form of disengagement/activity theories, but also of the biomedical paradigm and the world economic crises of the 1970s. As Phillipson (1998) points out, in the United Kingdom huge blocks of social expenditure were allocated to older people. Consequently, not only were older people viewed in medical terms but in resource terms by governments. This brought a new perception to attitudes to age and aging. In the United Kingdom, the William Beveridge post–World War II vision of universal access to welfare services was under sustained attack. As Phillipson (1998, 17) teases out: "Older people came to be viewed as a burden on western economies, with demographic change . . . seen as creating intolerable pressures on public expenditure."

A major concern of "political economy of old age" thinking was to challenge both the epistemological dominance of functionalist thought and the biomedical models of age and aging. The political economy approach wanted to have "an understanding of the character and significance of variations in the treatment of the aged, and to relate these to polity, economy and society in advanced capitalist society" (Estes 1986, 7).

The major focus is an interpretation of the relationship between aging and the economic structure. In the United States, political economy of old age was pioneered in the work of Caroll L. Estes (1979) and Min-kler and Estes (1998), for example. Similarly, in the United Kingdom, the work of Alan Walker (1981, 1985), Peter Townsend (1981), and Chris Phillipson (1982, 1998) added a critical sociological dimension to understanding age and ageing in advanced capitalist societies. For Estes (1979) the class structure is targeted as the key determinant of the position of older people in capitalist society. For Minkler and Estes (1998), political economy challenges the ideology of older people as belonging to a homogenous group unaffected by dominant structures in society.

Estes and Associates (2001) claim political economy focuses upon an analysis of the state in contemporary societal formations. Here, we can see how Marxism is interconnected to this theory. Estes and Associates (2001) look to how the state decides and dictates who is allocated re-sources and who is not. This impinges upon retirement and subsequent pension schemes.

Phillipson (1982, 1998) supplements this by suggesting that the retire-ment experience, linked to the timing of reduction of wages and enforced withdrawal from work, has put many older people in the U.K. in a finan-cially insecure position. Hence, the state can make and break the fortunes of its populace. Consequently, current governmental discourses about cutting public expenditure on pensions and increasingly calling for pri-vate provision of support for the aged legitimizes the ideological mystifi-cation stereotypes of "burden" groups and populations. This is a case of the state using its power to transfer responsibility of pension provision from the state and onto individuals. Indeed, blaming people for nonpro-vision of their own savings obscures and mystifies the fact that real eco-nomic problems derive from the capitalist mode of production and polit-ical decisions.

We can see that political economy is a "grand" theory drawing from Marxian historiography; it locates the determining explanatory factors in the structure of society and focuses upon welfare and its contribution to the institutional decommodification of retired older people. Ageist atti-tudes toward older people and their often impoverished position are best explained by their loss of social worth resulting from the loss of their pro-ductive roles in a society that puts a premium on production (Estes, Swan, and Gerard 1982).

Townsend (1981) further observes that society creates the social prob-lems of old age through "structured dependency" embedded in institutional ageism: poverty due to lack of material resources, retirement policies, negative consequences of residential care, and passive forms of community care services. Townsend focuses on a "structural" perspective of "rules and resources" governing older people in advanced capitalism and wider social system.

Similarly, Alan Walker (1981) has argued passionately for a political economy of old age in order to understand the marginal position of older people. In particular, Walker (1981, 77) paid attention to the "social creation of dependency" and how social structure and relations espoused by the mode of production helps intensify structural class marginalization. In a similar vein, Phillipson (1982, 1988) considers how capitalism helps socially construct the social marginality of older people in key areas such as welfare delivery. The important argument to be made is that inequalities in the distribution of resources should be understood in relation to the distribution of power within society and social class, rather than in terms of individual variation.

Political economy still retains an influence in gerontological theorizing but has reframed and renamed itself as "critical gerontology" (Phillipson 1998). Critical gerontology is a perspective whereby genuine knowledge is based on the involvement of the "objects" of study in its definition and results in a positive vision of how things might be better, rather than an understanding of how things actually are (Phillipson 1998). As suggested, "critical gerontology" grew out of political economy of old age; political economy was criticized for being overly concerned with "structured dependency" (Walker 1981) brought on by social and economic disadvantage and its implicit determinism that can see older people as passive, even insentient beings. Critical gerontology is still concerned with structural inequalities, but it is interested in moral concepts; it has a commitment not only to understanding marginality but also to challenging it. A reflexive critical gerontology also pays more attention to human agency and social class and the way in which individuals both influence the world around them and modify their behavior in response to information from the world in neoliberal contemporary modernity.

For example, from the 1980s on, the neoliberal dominance in social policy has been very successful because it has identified existential concepts such as self-responsibility, self-governance, and self-care that are said to facilitate social action (Leonard 1997). The regulation of personal conduct has shifted from being presented as "structured dependency" by the state (Walker 1981) to the responsibility of "older people" as "consumers" (Phillipson 1998). Since the 1980s, the nature of society is contested hotly by neoliberalism, with its central belief in the virtue of small government, especially in the economic sphere of life. For Estes, Biggs, and Phillipson (2004) the perception for neoliberals is that governments should intervene in markets only when the intervention is less damaging than the consequences of market failure. Where intervention is needed, it should be the minimum possible. If feasible, neoliberal governments should retain market exchanges in social welfarism. Quasi-market solutions should be favored over command solutions. The direct assumption of responsibility for the production of goods and services by government is almost never accepted except for the few special exemptions such as: national defense and maintaining law and order.

Under neoliberalism, the state reinvents itself and its welfare subjects based upon minimal intervention and regulation via a rolling program of privatization, deregulation, and contraction of welfare services (Estes and Associates 2001). Within the "mixed economy of welfare," there has been the social construction of a market-oriented, consumer-based approach to the delivery of care. As Peter Leonard (1997) claims, the neoliberal state is being reorganized to include a retention of a strong center to formulate policy but with the dissemination of responsibility for policy implementation to managerial regimes. As Gordon (1991, 36) points out: "The fulfillment of the liberal idea . . . is a recasting of the interface between the state and society to one of market order. It becomes the ambition of neo-liberalism to implicate individuals as players into the market game administered by managerial actors."

Such a development is framed in the language of the market, as opposed to social scientific discourse, although negative stereotyping can be brought in from time to time to reinforce an individualized or stigmatized notion of structured dependency. New neoliberal policy priorities on consumerism require new technologies if they are to influence both the control of resources and the "hearts and minds" of their objects. But for Chris Phillipson (1998), consumerist ideas in modern society ignore the experiences of older people, especially with regard to poverty and social deprivation. This is an enduring theme. After engaging in a series of qualitative and quantitative observations on older people in preindustrial and industrial societies, Powell (2001c) portrays a sense of the abandonment of the role of older people in neoliberal society. Modernity has failed to give due recognition to older people; the older you become, the more you experience a sense of relative deprivation. Fundamentally, the risk of hardship for the aging in modernity is exacerbated through neoliberal ideas of cutting state finance and enforcing people to use their own funds in the management of their own welfare. Indeed, Powell (2000) claims that neoliberalism at surface level consistently equates self-responsibility with freedom and sees people as active agents in consumer market. However, social class as a structural shaper and mover of society may leave many poorer older people in a vulnerable, "choiceless" position in social welfare; despite the neoliberal menu of rights, self-responsibility, and "freedoms" equated with becoming a "responsible consumer." Both the Blair and Bush governments have spoken about the need for private pensions and has constantly reinforced this point by saying that effects of an "ageing population" will mean that public finances could not fund a full pension, and older people and families must be more "responsible" with saving for pensions (Powell and Wahidin 2004). However, we have seen the effect of private pension schemes, especially in the United Kingdom; a report by the Office of Fair Trading (1997) found that up to £4 billion had been lost by pensioners in private pension schemes, according to the *Times* "the greatest financial scandal of the century." Then came the discovery after the death of Robert Maxwell that he had embezzled £400 million from his companies' pension schemes (Powell and Wahidin 2004).

"Critical gerontology" has had an enormous impact on theorizing about aging in recent years (Phillipson 1998). This approach to capitalist societies' treatment of older people has overemphasized class relations (Turner 1989) and neglected the differences between capitalist societies (Boneham and Blakemore 1994). More recently, attention has been paid to ways in which capitalist societies structure age relations in terms of gender (Arber and Ginn 1991, 1995) and race and ethnicity (Boneham and Blakemore 1994). Indeed, this theoretical approach reifies "older age" by discounting the potential for improvements in the social situation of older people (Featherstone and Hepworth 1993). Further, Wahidin and Powell (2003) ask why macrotheory overlooks both ontological and epistemological issues associated with the "aging body."

This is an important question that will be addressed in chapter 4.

FEMINIST INTERPRETATIONS OF AGING AND GENDER

In recent years, there has been an acceleration of feminist insights into understanding age and gender as entwined identity variables of analysis (Arber and Ginn 1991, 1995). There are two important issues: first, power imbalances shape theoretical construction; second, a group's place within the social structure influences the theoretical attention that they are afforded. Therefore, because older women tend to have lower-class status, especially in terms of economics, than men of all ages and younger women, they are given less theoretical attention (Arber and Ginn 1995). Although in recent years there has been a small but growing body of evidence, in mainstream sociological theory the interconnection of age and gender has been undertheorized and overlooked. In recent years, there has been an acceleration of feminist insights into understanding age and gender as identity variables of analysis (Arber and Ginn 1991, 1995). Finch (1986) agrees that the epistemological failure to incorporate women into mainstream theoretical perspectives on aging is a reflection of resistance to incorporating women into society and hence into sociological research.

"Mainstream" here refers to dominant theories in the sociological field, such as functionalist and political economy of old age theories, whose proponents could be accused of being "gender blind." As Arber and Ginn (1995) point out, there exists a tiny handful of feminist writers who take the topic of age seriously in understanding gender.

According to Acker (1988, cited in Arber and Ginn 1991), in all known societies the relations of distribution and production are influenced by gender and thus take on a gendered meaning. Gender relations of distribution in capitalist society are historically rooted and are transformed as the means of production change. Similarly, age relations are linked to the capitalist mode of production and relations of distribution. "Wages" take on a specific meaning depending on age. For example, teenagers work for less money than adults, who in turn work for less money than middle-aged adults. Further, young children rely on personal relations with family figures such as parents. Many older people rely on resources distributed by the state.

Older women are viewed as unworthy of respect or consideration (Arber and Ginn 1991). Catherine Itzin claims the double standard of aging arises from sets of conventional expectations as to age-pertinent attitudes and roles for each sex, which apply in patriarchal society.

These are defined by Itzin as a male and a female "chronology," socially defined and sanctioned so that the experience of prescribed roles is sanctioned by disapproval. Male chronology hinges on employment, but a woman's age status is defined in terms of events in the reproductive cycle (Itzin 1986).

It is perhaps emblematic of contemporary Western society that aging marginalizes the experiences of women through an interconnected oppression of gender and aging. The reason for this, as Arber and Ginn (1991) claim, is that patriarchal society exercises power through the chronologies of employment and reproduction, and through the sexualized promotion of a "youthful" appearance in women. This has been shown to be correct in terms of job segregration, marginalization, powerlessness, and the "double jeopardy" of being a woman and being old. Arguably, Arber and Ginn (1991, 1995) maintain that, because women's value is exercised, the awareness of a loss of a youthful appearance brings social devaluation; vulnerability to pressure is penetrated by cosmeticization. Indeed, the "beauty industrial complex" makes huge profit by articulating "anti-aging" creams and other products. It is estimated that L'Oreal has an annual turnover of $9.4 billion on anti-aging products (Powell 2002). Further, Mary Daly (cited in Arber and Ginn 1991) draws a mirror image between Western cosmetic surgery and the genital mutilation carried out in some African societies: both cultured practices demonstrate the pressure on women to comply with male standards of desirability and the extent of male domination. For older black women, the ideal of "beauty" portrayed by white male culture was doubly distant and alienating, until growing black consciousness subverted disparaging language and argued "black is beautiful" through resistance to patriarchal and racist power relations.

Gender and Marginality in Old Age

In the United States, women comprise 59 percent of those over sixty-five; they account for 72 percent of the older poor (Powell 2001b). According to Estes and Associates (2001), the poverty rate in the United States is 19 percent, of which older women are the poorest social group. In 1993 older women's average income was 43 percent lower than that of older men. Poorest of all are older black women, with 82 percent classified as poor or "near poor." Indeed, for many women, such negative financial conditions would express powerlessness and economic marginalization. Many older women's adverse financial situations came about because their participation in the labor market was limited and dominated by men, thus generating "dependency" upon men. In terms of social security benefits, 66 percent of older women received benefits below the poverty line. Further, the work of Janet Finch (1986) has problematized the construction of social services in Western society for poorer older women by describing how such services contribute to dominant discursive constructions of older women as "incapable" and "dependent."

While feminist theorizing in gerontology continues to raise important questions relating to aging and gender, there are other identity variables that are still given scant attention, a problem that is replicated across functionalism, critical gerontology, and feminist modern theories. In order to address this, the next section explores two issues—race and sexuality—which are important to consider if the full complexity of the processes surrounding modernist discourses of aging are to be understood and appreciated.

RACE AND AGING

According to Powell and Longino (2002) issues of ethnicity in social gerontology have been scarcely researched. First, social gerontology could highlight the significance of cultural values, ethnic traditions, and a sense of belonging to a group with shared experiences in which older individuals may ground their identities. Second, the experience of black older people of being a minority within a minority is important. An examination of the minority concept raises questions about the validity of supposed majority "white" norms. Third, the experiences of minority ethnic groups in trying to obtain social justice and fairness in terms of health care, for example, expose the ethnocentrist nature of social welfare in Western culture.

Boneham and Blakemore (1994) claim that the dominant theories of age and aging need to be reconsidered with racial diversity in mind. Such views of macrotheories of functionalism, political economy, and feminism have ignored the experiences of older black people (Patel 1990).

Further, the biomedical model has discussed how the aging body has declined and has attempted to discover variations through different explanations of the body in different cultures. For example, Stuart Hall

(1992) has considered how scientific definitions of "race" are racist and somehow attempt to explain physical characteristics of people and behaviors. Compounding the decline model with inferior/superior scientific discourses generates what Sim (1990) has called "metaphors of pathology," which seep into Western society to engender what Hall (1992) calls different "historical forms of racisms." According to Hall (1992), racism in Western culture is linked with colonialism and slavery, legacies of the history of the Enlightenment and industrial capitalism in the U.K., United States, and Europe. Conceptually, the concept of "race" refers to a "category composed of individuals who share biologically transmitted traits that members of a society deem socially significant" (Saraga 1998, 324). A critical perspective goes underneath the surface to raise critical questions about categories or types of people based on classification. "Racism" refers to the idea that one racial category is innately superior or inferior to another. Therefore, the assertion of one specific category of individuals over others has served as a powerful tool for relegating the targets of taunts to a status of social inferiority.

According to Patel (1990) the "economic and social conditions of older black people can be explained away by 'blaming the victim.' The focus on such arguments then shifts from individual pathology to family deficiency to cultural defects."

Indeed, Simon Biggs (1993) claims the myth of "looking after one's own" is replicated by professional and institutional practices and services. Biggs (1993) sees the deficiencies in the system that are at fault but the "passing of the buck" by the system is to pathologize stereotypical views that "it's their fault" if they do not provide for their own.

The assumption that ethnic communities are made up entirely of caring, close-knit, extended families that do not require outside care and support has meant that the state, both local and central, has failed to meet the needs of population groups that run along ethnic lines. For example, despite the growing proportion of older black people, very few attend local day care centers or residential care. They are often put off, partly by the absence of other black service users and by the predominance of Western ideologies and traditions regarding activities and fare (Bond and Coleman 1990). Similarly, Wing Au (1996, cited in Powell 2001b) found that among the older Chinese community in Liverpool, Great Britain, social service departments were very slow to meet their care needs because they thought "they looked after their own." This highlights a restricted view of culture in which the concept of normalization causes the system to overlook the very people whom social services should be treating.

Open racism continues to exist. Hall (1992) claims that black older people are subjected to racist abuse and experienced hostility from white older people. Patel (1990, 39) claims that "sufficient importance may not be attached to instances of racial abuse in a home . . . because staff involved deem it as insignificant or because white elders cannot be expected to change their behaviour. Hence black elders must put up with racism or not use the service." Indeed, according to Alcock (1996), there exists institutional racism in the British National Health Service in that older black people are not treated by medical staff, including nurses and doctors, the same as older white people. Indeed, not only are there serious questions about health disadvantage coupled with this, but also the manifestation of "elder abuse" is not detected and consequently many older black people do not have their concerns, needs, or situations addressed. Furthermore, Boneham and Blakemore (1994) suggest that the problems faced by older men and women from both Asian and Afro-Caribbean communities are posed in terms of the devaluation of old age in Western culture, based on consumer demand and reflecting racial disadvantage by a lack of adequate social facilities.

Culture itself can be silencing for many older black people. Hazan (1980, cited in Boneham and Blakemore 1994) compiled a study of an older Jewish community and found that many older people found it painful to talk about memories of the past such as the Holocaust but were dismissed by white professional health workers who had no comparable experience—which in turn created distrust and anxiety.

SEXUALITY AND AGING

The issue of sexuality has been marginal to modernist theories of aging. The oldest gay men and lesbians have few, if any, positive role models for coupling, aging, or creating alternative family structures (Isay 1996; Fullmer 1995). Fullmer explains that people "coming out" later in life must integrate themselves into a new culture and may be faced with some of the same tasks that typically confront adolescents and young adults, and that the age of coming out could influence family structure and support systems. This indicates that the later in life a person comes out, the more difficult it is to integrate into a gay/lesbian social network or restructure the family system one is in to allow for the gay/lesbian relationship (Isay 1996). Fullmer remarks that now that more gay and lesbian couples have the opportunity to adopt children, they may have children and grandchildren who may be more accepting of them and are there to support them in their old age. Gay men or lesbians who have gone from a heterosexual relationship to a homosexual one might encounter more problems with their biological children accepting their sexuality at a time when they may need them the most (Saraga 1998).

Families of older gay and lesbian people have many of the same strengths and deal with the same issues as other families. But along with getting older, they also have to face the prejudices of being gay or lesbian (Fullmer 1995). "Older gays and lesbians have learned through a lifetime of experience that they will likely be discriminated against if it is known that they are homosexual. It is common in our society to typify older gay men and lesbians as pathetic and lonely 'dirty old men' or 'child molesters,' as 'old maids' or as 'drag queens'" (Fullmer 1995, 66). Gay and lesbian couples and their families may be alienated from institutions such as churches because many religious organizations have been very vocal in their condemnation of homosexuality (Fullmer 1995).

Public retirement housing does not allow "unrelated adults" to live under the same roof. This includes nursing homes and private retirement centers, which can make assumptions that their residents are heterosexual and structure activities on the basis of these assumptions (Isay 1996). Hospitals often have policies that allow only "immediate" family members to be in the rooms of seriously ill patients and help make decisions for them. It is also not uncommon for biological family members to contest a will that names a homosexual partner as the beneficiary and win, because there is no legally defined relationship between the partners (Dalley 1988).

The major sociological issue and lesson to be learned here is how to overcome the impact of class, race, and gender without merely adding more identity formations, such as race and sexuality, to the task of understanding aging in modernity.

CONCLUSION: DECONSTRUCTING
MODERNIST THEORIES OF AGING

Taken together, different yet modernist theories of aging consisting of functionalism, critical gerontology, and feminist gerontology have helped shape important debates about the extent and nature of an "aging" society. Such social theories have been used also to analyze pressing social issues such as the engagement of older people with society, active aging, pension politics, and the gendered nature of aging in modernity. However, the concerns of these theoretical resources have been primarily macro-oriented: for example, the political economy approach overemphasizes structural disadvantage (cf. Walker 1985) or "structured dependency" (Townsend 1981) at the expense of focus to older people's sense of human agency in, for example, fighting for political and economic representation through social organization (Tulle 2004).

Such modernist models of aging, by focusing upon the social problems of older people, may have taken up, promoted, and reinforced the "ageism" which many are arguing against (Bytheway 1995). Consequently, modernist epistemologies of aging can be regarded as overarching explanations of aging. Thus one finds diversity, subjectivity, and microdimensions of aging in the lifestyles and experiences of older people.

Indeed, a pressing question may be, what makes such theories modernist? They are modernist in the sense that they have afforded "grand narratives" to aging. For example, they supply macrogeneralizations to their area of social concern: "in the interests of capitalism" and "in the interests of patriarchy." For Powell and Longino (2002) an alternative form of theorizing drawn from postmodernism suggests that "grand theories" place too many limits on what is conceptually possible regarding aging and that it is too totalized. The objectification of older people that is implied by the term "social class" and "gender" relegates individuals to socially constructed categories. Likewise, the Marxist notion of "false consciousness" fails to recognize that this can be patronizing to many people who resist social marginalization. For Featherstone and Hepworth (1993), individual experiences are no longer believed to be determined by such social constructs such as "class." A postmodern perspective has tended to take a critical stance relative to Marxist developments. It attempts instead to tease out ontologically flexible depictions of aging, and it questions the truth claims behind ontological and epistemological generalizations based on "concrete" social divisions such as race, class, and gender, which are touchstones of modern gerontological theories (Biggs 1999).

The next chapter focuses on postmodern constructions of aging that alternatively emphasize the cultural interaction between the aging body and social context in shaping the way people experience their lifetimes. Even though lives are seen as embedded in social relationships, popular culture, and history, the notion of the "aging body" is an important narrative in the social construction of aging identity. This view has rich epistemological and ontological implications in terms of understanding the aging self and social reality. It draws upon attempts to overcome the aging body as articulated by biomedical gerontology. In terms of identity, we are talking about the possibilities of reinvention and denial of limits. In many ways this approach also reflects the "outside-looking-in" perspective insofar as, as social theory, aging is bounded by the internal-external duality and the possibilities that the external makes available. The reterritorialization of the aging body by society, and paradigmatically by postmodern social theory, is a strategy that parallels the denial of subjectivity within the main traditions of the biomedical model. It is within this *postmodern imaginative* space that an understanding of the aging body may take place.

II

POSTMODERN
DECONSTRUCTIONS OF AGING

4

Postmodernism, Culture, and the Aging Body

INTRODUCTION

In the previous chapter we interrogated modernist and macrotheories of aging comprising functionalism, political economy of old age, and feminist gerontology, which maintained that aging is reduced to disengagement/activity and social roles and affected not only by capitalism and economic forces but also by patriarchy and the exploitation of all women by men. It can be suggested that such modernist theories, by focusing on the bigger picture of life, exclude social relations at the microtexture of everyday life. This is not to deny the important and critical points that have been made by the sociological theories discussed in the previous chapter. Indeed, such approaches are significant to pointing to emergence of social problems of aging as cast through the socioeconomic gaze.

Notwithstanding this, and despite the consolidation of these important theories of aging, there was no specific innovative theoretical development with a specific focus on an understanding of the "body." Although functionalism and political economy have their theoretical differences, they both focused on structures to the exclusion of the body. The contentious point to make here is that, by ignoring the sense of "lived experiences" of older people, all modernist theories provide perceptions of adult aging that are overgeneralized.

Understanding aging bodies plays a crucial part in the identity formation of older people in the representations of the body. Outside of gerontology, feminism has focused on the ways *younger* women's bodies were controlled and dominated within patriarchy. According to Twigg (2000), feminism has focused our attention as to how women represent the body itself. The current interest in the body and embodiment in social and human sciences encompasses a range of themes and theoretical traditions (Powell 2001c). Historically, the discipline of sociology ignored the centrality of the body in terms of its prioritized "rational" or scientific analysis of modern social systems (Oberg and Tornstam 1999; Wahidin and Powell 2001). Indeed, the sociological tradition has focused upon the social forces that impinge upon the construction of personal biographies and the society in which sociologists live (Mills 1959). The sociological aspirations of Karl Marx, Emile Durkheim, and Max Weber distanced them from a study of the body in order to generate intellectual respectability to ideas about social order and social change (Turner 1989). Sociology simultaneously distanced itself from biological reductionism, which, as part of the "project of modernity," attempted to talk of the body as an object to be predicted and controlled. Coupled with this, the modernist preoccupation with theorizing and constructing grand narratives in theories of aging has also tended to exclude an analysis of the body. As Powell (2001b) points out, theorizing occupies a commanding position in sociological analysis; with a preoccupation with abstraction, bodies are things to be transcended or ignored.

Moreover, gerontology continues to be in the thrall of a biomedical discourse on aging (Powell and Longino 2001); although concerned with the fixed limitations of the aging body, it restricts an ontologically flexible understanding of aging. Conversely, we can question how the aging body acquires meaning, and also how the meaningful body itself, in its turn, influences and limits signifying processes and social efforts as related to society and culture.

The central focus is not on the body as a natural given, or as the conglomerate of neurons, hormones, and genes, but rather as a concrete social and cultural practice of everyday life. Traditionally, the body in its actual realities has been generally neglected within the social sciences and humanities (Shilling 1993; Katz 1996). The investigation of the body was more or less relegated to biology and the medical sciences. In recent years, however, the body has made a major comeback within all realms of scholarly and scientific research (Shilling 1993)—especially those fields that have traditionally focused on the "inanimate" aspects of reality. For example, literary critics, film theorists, political scientists, historians have shown an upsurge in interest in a variety of "bodily matters"—that is, in the concrete, corporeal dimensions of that which renders us all recognizable human beings, the physical aspects of our individual and collective embodied specificity and experiences.

It is by querying the role of the body that one can move away from the modernist biomedical approach, which locates the body within the naturalistic framework (Powell and Longino 2001). The postmodern perspective adds a richness to the literature by examining embodiment and the corporeality of the body in all its social guises (Wahidin and Powell 2001, 2003). It places the body not as a passive materiality that is acted upon but one that negotiates the capillaries of power, enabling itself to be always in the process of becoming through the experiences of embodiment (Longino and Powell 2004). Moreover, in a postmodern culture, the prospect of an endless life has been revived through consumer images of perpetual youth and the blurring of traditional life-course boundaries (Featherstone and Hepworth 1993).

Therefore, this chapter focuses on such themes as conceptualizing postmodernism; theorizing the aging body; popular culture and aging body; gendered bodies, and finally biotechnologies and the reconstruction of aging bodies.

THE DEVELOPMENT OF POSTMODERN SOCIAL THEORY

The episteme of postmodernism represents a decisive break with modernity (Delanty 1999; Powell and Longino 2002). Postmodernism emerged from Western social theory; the debate was instigated by Derrida, Baudrillard, and Lyotard in the tradition of the modern and calls for breaks within this tradition. This is clearly illustrated by the work of French postmodern theorist Baudrillard, who adopted an extreme abandonment of Enlightenment values in his devastating critique of modernist approaches in sociology. Baudrillard focuses on the transcendental nature of society through the concept of hyperreality. He argued that in modern society there is no distinction between reality and illusion (Seidman 1994; May 1996) and that individuals live their lives through a simulation of reality. Nothing has any true origin or authenticity, and lived experience is itself a mere construction, made of a series of depthless signs and representations (Smart 1993, 52). In this way Baudrillard argues that sociology can no longer serve a political purpose, because power relations have been dispersed through the hyperreal nature of society (Smart 1993, 55). The "neat divisions," "hierarchies," and "foundational premises" of both modernity and sociology (Seidman 1994, 347) are no longer relevant. In particular, Baudrillard rejects the economic determinism of Marxism and states that there are no longer such fundamental systems of exploitation, only superficial simulations and exchanges (May 1996):

> Like the philosopher Nietzsche, Baudrillard criticizes such claims to truth and favours a model based on what he calls seduction. Seduction plays on the surface: it is the surface appearance that is effective in determining action, not some latent or hidden structure as claimed by Marxism or Freudianism. (Thompson 1992, 244)

For Lyotard (1984) the project of modernity has become obsolete and society had entered the "postmodern condition." Lyotard deconstructs the way in which bodies of knowledge are created in order to legitimate hierarchical structures in society. In his influential work *The Postmodern Condition* (1984, first published in French in 1979), Lyotard looked at the changes that have occurred to the nature of "knowledge" throughout history. He pointed to how premodern society was based on narratives that were made up of religion and myth (Seidman 1994, 206). Knowledge was a body of stories that were thought to explain the way society was and determine that which was "good" or "evil." In this way such narratives legitimated the social rules of behavior that determined how society was structured and who had authority (Seidman 1994, 206). In contrast, modernity, Lyotard argued, was thought to be based on "true" knowledge that rejected the "narratives" of premodernity. However, in *The Postmodern Condition,* Lyotard asserts that in actual fact supposedly "pure," "real" scientific knowledge is also self-legitimating, so is itself merely another "narrative" (McLennan 1992, 332). Lyotard argues that scientific thought and knowledge have political and philosophical agendas and are therefore value laden and not totally objective (McLennan 1992, 333). An ideal that underpinned the beginnings of Enlightenment thought was that the attainment of absolute knowledge for all would mean the attainment of absolute freedom for all (May 1996).

It was thought that knowledge was the key to breaking down power structures that had existed during the domination of premodern narratives. But Lyotard pointed to the contradictions within modern scientific bodies of knowledge and argued that they are themselves still made up of hierarchical power structures. Just as in earlier societies narratives served to determine who had the right to speak and who did not, Lyotard states, this is still the case. Hierarchies still operate and serve to give the decision-making elite the power to decide what gets defined as legitimate knowledge.

> Countless scientists have seen their "move" ignored or repressed, sometimes for decades, because it too abruptly destabilized the accepted positions, not only in the university and scientific hierarchy, but also in the problematic. (Lyotard 1984, 63)

Lyotard argues, therefore, that science can no longer be seen as a unified body working toward the emancipation of humanity (Longino and Powell 2004). His ideas can be linked to those of Nietzsche, who believes that "truth" and "knowledge" are merely a matter of conventions that falsify and dissimulate to promote human survival (May 1996). Rather than being a grand quest for universal laws, Lyotard argues, knowledge is sought in order to keep human society functioning efficiently (Steuerman 1992, 108). The assertion by science that it is constantly objectively striving for truth and progress is called into question by the fact that the search for knowledge is inextricably linked to achieving economic growth in society (McLennan 1992, 332). That is not to say that these two things are incompatible, but rather to question if the search for truth and progress can ever be totally objective when there is a financial incentive. Lyotard argues that those involved in striving for progress "allocate our lives for the growth of power. In matters of social justice and of scientific truth alike, the legitimation of that power is based on its optimizing the system's performance—efficiency" (Lyotard 1984, xxiv).

Since, as Lyotard (1984) points out, the legitimation of science can be called into question, knowledge as a unified, overarching metanarrative (such as the Enlightenment narrative that knowledge equals liberation, as was key in modernity) breaks down into a wide range of "micronarratives" (Lyotard 1984, xxiv). Each separate specialism has a different discourse and plays different "language games" in an attempt to gain accreditation from its specific audience (Seidman 1994, 208; Lyotard 1984, 64).

This, to Lyotard is what ultimately characterizes the "Postmodern Condition."

Lyotard's rejection of grand narratives obviously has strong implications for the structure of social gerontology. By rejecting the belief in the ability to universalize, philosophical thought loses its authority to make any suggestions as to what action can be taken in order to make changes in society (Smart 1993, 37). In response to the criticisms of the Enlightenment made by Lyotard, Habermas wishes to consolidate the "project of modernity" and further argues that we should not completely abandon the possibility of a rational pursuit of truth (Steuerman 1992, 107). He defends modernity and argues that what is needed is more philosophical discussion, not less (Steuerman 1992, 113). Habermas states that through the use of communicative action, language, and rational dialogue, the Enlightenment aims of truth, justice, and freedom are still attainable alongside social consensus (Steuerman 1992, 104–7). However, Lyotard argues that Habermas ignores the fact that communication cannot simply take the form of consensual, rational dialogue; it will always take place in the context of power struggles (Powell and Biggs 2000).

Therefore, rather than holding on to the ideals of Enlightenment scientific thought, Lyotard might suggest that we attempt to "restructure" social theory (and social gerontology) in a postmodern vein so that we might find a democratic, pluralistic solution (Seidman 1994, 207). He argued that while grand narratives, such as the Marxian narrative of class conflict, were well intentioned and essential to modernist social theory, to continue to utilize such concepts fails adequately to challenge the hierarchical structures in society and therefore continues to marginalize and repress issues of difference.

"Postmodernism abandons absolute standards, universal categories and grand theories in favour of local, contextualized, and pragmatic conceptual strategies" (Seidman 1994, 207). Seidman outlines the postmodern idea that the splintering of metanarratives has occurred to such an extent that society has become decentered. That is, there is no longer a common unifying culture in existence (Seidman 1994, 206). Individuals experience their lives at constantly shifting intersections of different discourses and language games. Instances of oppression, therefore, occur in many different contexts as individuals constantly construct, deconstruct, and reconstruct themselves in terms of these "fractured identities" (Powell 2000). Indeed, Lyotard argues that a postmodern analysis does offer a way of explaining issues of multiplicity and difference (Lyotard 1984, 81).

Powell and Longino (2002) suggest that there are several themes that are shared in postmodern analysis of aging, which consolidate Baudrillard's, Lyotard's and Seidman's theoretical excursions. First, there is distrust in the concept of absolute and objective truth. "Truth" is viewed as contextual, situational, and conditional (Biggs and Powell 2001). Second, emphasis is placed on fragmentation rather than universalism, again pushing away from the general and toward the particular (Powell 2001b). Third, local power is preferred over the centralized power of the nation-state, and *de*centralization, or the process of democratization of power, is a pervasive theme of postmodern narratives (Powell and Longino 2001). Fourth, reality is simulated but is otherwise not held to be a very meaningful concept; reality conceived as a general and universal truth is profoundly doubted (Powell and Longino 2002). Fifth, we are seeing the rise and consolidation of consumer culture that tends to put "power" in the hands of the consumers but can also equally manipulate consumers through marketing ploys and interpolating discourses of consumer freedom by dictating costs in the global marketplace (Biggs and Powell 2001). Finally, diversity and difference are emphasized and valued above commonality based on homogeneity (Powell 2001b; May 1996). Postmodern analysis of culture is no longer a fringe perspective inasmuch as it apparently promotes strategies of individualism and diversity, and postmodernism is critical of strategies that devalue individuals because of any characteristic that would control access to knowledge and could thereby assault identity (Biggs and Powell 2001). In ethics, as in epistemology, the final result is a kind of moral relativism (Longino and Powell 2004).

Central to postmodern assertions is that in the twenty-first century there has occurred a radical shift in the constitution of social order, paralleling the significance of the Enlightenment and birth of modernity that led to the emergence of the biomedical sciences and social sciences in general. This new sociocultural formation has been termed postmodernity and is seen as to be characterized by increasing diversity and the loosening of structural modernist principles. Postmodern thought may be seen as a revolt against both the structural version of gerontology theory—political economy and feminism—and as a break with the rigidity and certainties of the positivist or biomedical strand of gerontology. All forms of meaning and "knowledge" are rendered problematic and no longer to be taken for granted as the myth of the biomedical objectivity is debunked. Hence, the controversial point is that modernist sociological theories claim the same forms of certainty, universalism, and rigidity that are seen as master narratives of positivism. For example, political economy of aging (cf. Estes 1979) emphasizes the importance of economic materiality, applicable to every older person in North America. But this has also been conflated with the biomedical obsession with an objective social world that was to be scientifically knowable. Although the political foundations of these very two different "modernist" explanations are diametrically opposed, they are treated as one in treating aging as an "object" to be predicted or problematized.

THEORIZING THE AGING BODY

Postmodern discussions relating to the aging body in social gerontology are slowly developing (Powell and Longino 2002). While the "body" as a concept implies an objectified and "natural" entity, the body is now beginning to be viewed as increasingly complex. The importance of the body to gerontology is in many ways obvious. For example, illness can limit the "normal" functioning of the body, and this can have profound psychological, political, and social consequences that interest gerontologists of all backgrounds. Moreover, health is often thought of in terms of body maintenance, and such activities form a pivotal feature of consumer societies. However—and despite consumer culture inscribing and disseminating negative ideas about aging bodies—at a personal level the age one appears to be may be different from the age one actually is, as though one is wearing a disguise. Featherstone and Hepworth (1993) maintain that old age is a mask that "conceals the essential identity of the person beneath" (148). That is, while the external appearance is changing with age, the essential identity is not, so that the difference between physical appearance and the unchanging image in his or her head may surprise the aging individual. Bytheway and Johnson (1998) assert that we need a well-constituted image of what "old" looks like before we could recognize the signs in our own images. Thompson (1992) argues that people derive their sense of identity in later life from the achievements of the past and what remains to be accomplished in the future, rather than from a set of stereotypical—usually negative—attributes of old age. Unless they are ill or depressed, old people do not feel old "inside." Furthermore, old people tend to associate old age with the residents of nursing homes, an image from which they want to distance themselves (Biggs 1999).

Simultaneously, the aging body has been exploited by popular consumer culture, which has attempted to colonize narratives afforded to the aging body (Longino and Powell 2004). Morris (1998) agrees, asserting that consumer culture is preoccupied with reconstructing aging bodies, promoted through the glamorized representations of advertising. The visual image is increasingly dominant in Western culture; images can also be used to disseminate alternative constructions of old age. In their analysis of retirement magazines, Featherstone and Hepworth (1993) argue that the types of images of old people presented in specialist magazines are consonant with attempts at focusing on the positive side of being old. This is usually linked to "young" old age, early retirement, and the continuation of full activities, usually through the engagement in leisure activities funded by careful financial planning. The message here is that there now exist opportunities for consumption (McAdams 1993; Gilleard and Higgs 2000) and enjoyment in old age that act as a counterpoint to traditional images of old people inexorably driven toward death via senility, physical decrepitude, loneliness, and disengagement. Thus, consumer society reinforces negative language and images of later life; in turn, this can produce a slide into "symbolic" death (Powell and Longino 2001).

Indeed, postmodern gerontology would claim that life-course models that associate aging with both decline and universal stages of life are fundamentally flawed (Powell and Longino 2001). To exemplify the fluid and blurred nature of aging identity, a uni-age style, Meyrowitz (1984, cited in Featherstone and Hepworth 1993), argues that in Western society, "children" are becoming more like adults and adults more childlike. There is a growing similarity in modes of presentation of self, gestures and postures, fashions and leisure-time pursuits adopted by both parents and their children.

For Featherstone and Hepworth (1993) the private sphere of family life is becoming less private, as children are granted access to the larger world through popular media such as television and the Internet. Previously concealed aspects of adult life (such as sex, death, money, and problems besetting adults who are anxious about the roles and selves they present to children) are no longer so easy to keep secret. A uni-age behavioral style is influenced by the advent of media imagery that, as a powerful form of communication, bypasses the controls that adults once established over the kinds of information believed to be suitable for children. (An interesting premodern comparison relative to childhood resides with the work of Aries. He claims that in premodern times the child was allowed to participate as an adult after the age of seven.) One contribution of postmodern ideas is to illuminate the blurring of age identities in terms of "dress" and "work."

Therefore, the importance of the "body" to social gerontology is in many ways apparent. For example, the body in pain: illness can limit functions of the body and have effects that attract the interest of social gerontologists of all backgrounds globally. David B. Morris posits in his engaging study, *The Culture of Pain*: "Pain not only hurts but more often than not frustrates, baffles, and resists us. Yet it seems we cannot simply suffer pain but most always are compelled to make sense of it" (Morris 1991, 18).

Beyond the problem of making sense of pain (for example), the reason why the body is central to the discipline of social gerontology is that the *biomedical model* in particular has given intellectual respectability to "scientific" ideas concerning aging that raise issues about altering the boundaries of the physical body (Freund 1988). For example, biomedical science can reconstruct bodies through plastic surgery. Further, it can interfere with genetic structures; and it can swap internal organs from one human body to another (Haraway 1991; Powell and Longino 2001). "We," according to Haraway (1991), have become "cyborgs"—not wholly machines and not wholly natural organisms either. She argues: "Twentieth century machines have made thoroughly ambiguous the difference between natural and artificial, mind and body, self-developing and externally designed, and many other distinctions that used to apply to organisms and machines" (10).

However, Shilling (1993) argues that there is a schizophrenic ambivalence about the body: the more we know about bodies, and the more we are able to control, intervene, and restructure them, the more *uncertain* we become as to what the body really is. The boundaries between the physical body and society are becoming increasingly bifurcated. The body, like parchment, is written upon, inscribed by variables such as gender, age, sexual orientation, and ethnicity and by a series of inscriptions that are dependent on types of spaces and places. However, as Shilling (1993) powerfully argues, the more we know about bodies, the more we are able to govern and modify norms—

highlighting how gendered and ageist discourses serve to confine and define aging bodies.

The role of the body has become a discursive site of power to be produced, acted upon, and received. Sandra Bartky, for instance, has argued that "normative femininity is coming more and more to be centred on woman's body—not its duties and obligations or even its capacity to bear children, but its sexuality, more precisely its presumed heterosexuality and its appearance" (S. Bartky 1988, quoted in Wahidin and Powell 2003, 8).

One cannot argue in relation to body modification that the performance of the body is solely one to counter hegemonic biomedical discourses, or one based purely on aesthetic value, without fully encapsulating the varied and multifaceted technologies of the corporeal and the self. Through these bodily practices, old bodies are transforming their gendered habitus and thus creating identities for themselves that transgress the boundaries of how to manage old bodies (Longino and Powell 2004).

Bryan S. Turner (1995) emphasizes several key processes that work upon and within the body across time and space. Longino and Powell (2004) give as an example, here, how the effort to crack the genetic code of biological aging has directed attention away from socially determined life-chances in later life. Power relations become eclipsed by narratives of technological application subject to manipulation and control by a skilled professional. This is often a concern of medical students as they begin their education, but it is also often lost as part of their induction into a biomedical culture (Longino and Powell 2004).

Powell and Longino (2002) have argued that the disaggregation of the aging body takes a number of forms. First, the experience of aging is broken down into a number of separate age categories, each with its accompanying medical specialism. Second, the dominance of biomedical perspectives on aging has led to an acceptance of the association between adult aging and bodily and mental deterioration. Finally they note that a combination of specialism and a separation of mind from the body has compromised the gendered experience of bodily aging (Powell and Longino 2002). If aging becomes associated with illness, and the avoidance of aging with cure, then an expansion of medical discourse to include ever more aspects of the older person's life-world leaves two alternatives: subsumption of the self under the rubric of a sick body or a continual flight from the "symptoms" of aging (Longino and Powell 2004). Both depend upon biomedical hegemony (Biggs and

Powell 2001). It follows from the above analysis that a biomedical approach to aging encourages the evacuation of certain forms of experience, through the reclassification of experience into symptoms that can then be addressed separately from wider social impacts (Phillipson 1998).

Frank (1998) argues that the ability to tell one's own story of illness is by no means straightforward. If, as Foucault (1977) claims, the maintenance of existing power relations depends not on the use of force but on the ability to persuade active subjects to reproduce those relations for themselves, then the telling of narratives will always be suspect. Further, Frank (1996) poses the almost unanswerable question, When does self-care turn into a technology for producing a certain sort of self? For example, Estes, Biggs, and Phillipson (2003) suggest that personal narratives, particularly for older people in health settings, remain both a means of taking care of oneself and conformity to a restricted legitimizing discourse of their bodies and physical appearance.

Simultaneously, becoming, and being, old are about the corporeality of being old, the experience of holding on to physical/mental integrity and reasonable health (Baltes and Carstersen 1996). It is therefore important to focus on the construction of identity that is imposed upon the discourses of exteriority and interiority that impinge upon the body.

The postmodern interest in the body presents paradoxical aspects: the contemporary world, on the one hand, is obsessed by the body and its materiality, emphasized by the attention given over to it in the media and consumer society in general; on the other hand, it has emptied the body of its symbolic meaning. It is no coincidence that recent artistic performances (e.g., body art) and popular youth culture practices (e.g., body piercing) appear like a desperate and contradictory attempt to recover the ritual significance of the body. To examine historically the various theories about the body is to become aware that Western culture has always, in a Manichean manner, separated the material from the spiritual, the body from the soul (May 1996). Western philosophy, founded on the Platonic dichotomy between body and soul, has considered the body as a prison and tomb for the psyche. Intellect in the Platonic conception becomes an autonomous and independent entity (May 1996). This disjoining operation conceived the soul positively and the body, with its materiality, negatively. As May (1996) stresses, this paradox in Western culture is to be found at the origin of Greek civilization because, if philosophical thought tries to disregard the body because of its corporeality, it nevertheless returns as a metaphor for the representation of the political system. In place of this dichotomy, primitive communities have endowed the body with a polysemic meaning: the body was the center of a symbolic network that ensured that both the natural and social world were modeled on its possibilities. In this way, the body was never an isolated and single entity but always a cosmic one, part of a community. Every individual managed to preserve, by means of a dense circulation of symbols connecting the one with the whole, his/her own individual perception of the body, albeit within a range of multiplicities and differences. At a time when youthfulness is valued, the dislocation felt between the eternality of the body or the surfaces of the body that symbolize the self and the internality of the body leaves many to combat age through "maintaining" their bodies via the commodification of youth.

The performance of the body is indicative of how the body is a discursive site of power to be produced, acted upon, negotiated, and received. These techniques create the space for resistance, enabling power to be positive yet at the same time negative. It is the polysemic nature of the body in all its guises that the performance is not solely one to counter, resist, and subvert hegemonic biomedical discourses. It is rather a relationship encapsulating the multivaried technologies of corporeal and self inscriptions based on what went on before, the present and immediate past (Wahidin and Powell 2003).

In a postmodern culture, the prospect of an endless life has been revived through consumer images of perpetual youth and a blurring of traditional life-course boundaries (Featherstone and Hepworth 1993). Bauman (1992) posits of the "postmodern strategy of survival," compared to "traditional ways of dabbling with timelessness," that: "instead of trying (in vain) to colonize the future, it dissolves it in the present. It does not allow the finality of time to worry the living . . . by oscillating time (all of it, exhaustively, without residue) into short lived, evanescent episodes. It rehearses mortality, so to speak, by practicing it day by day" (Bauman 1992, 2).

POPULAR CULTURE AND AGING BODY

Throughout particular literary texts and through representations of the celebrated youthful body; the old body is something to be feared and resisted and thus at all costs should be held at bay (Longino and Powell 2004; Powell and Longino 2002).

For example, the motif of the woman's body transposed into a mythical and allegorical dimension returns in an essay on Irish women's literature in which Roberta Gefter Wondrich examines the contradictory relationship that women have with the images related to the myth of Ireland as a nation. On the one hand, Ireland is a great mother, a Marian Catholic image characterized by self-denial, an ever obedient woman who sacrifices herself for her son and is thus essentially passive; on the other hand, Ireland is the "old woman" who symbolizes the nation devastated by its destroyers (Greenblatt 1980).

The sense of isolation marks the works of a writer like Samuel Beckett, who uses the elderly body to express the absurdity of existence (Miller 1993). In several of his plays, Beckett represented old age through the violent divide between body and mind; he dramatized the inevitable physical decay of the body, until the only trace left of it on the stage is the word, the voice. Beckett studied and explored all the possible relations between the elderly body and space, between body and movement and between body and the objects that surround it. Beckett's ideal seems to be that of a man on a bicycle, a sort of a Cartesian centaur who emblematizes the phrase "mens sana in corpore disposito." In this respect the author explodes the dilemma "Cogito ergo sum": he rebels against the definition of man as a thinking machine (Miller 1993). Beckett's characters experience a tension between mind and body—a mind that is subject to continuous changes even if imprisoned in a body that is caught in a process of decaying and decrepitude. It is interesting to compare Beckett's characters with the disconcerting images of painter Francis Bacon, which are characterized by a prevailing sense of the vulnerability of man and, above all, his solitude, in the hell of the modern condition (Miller 1993). At the center of Bacon's representation is a view of man as a contingency, a creature with a disfigured face and body. This can be seen in his *Study after Velazquez's Portrait of Pope Innocent X* (1953), in which the theme of the cage and the imprisonment of the body underlines the horror of old age, emphasized by the screaming mouth of the figure (Greenblatt 1980).

Powell and Longino (2002) deal with some paradoxes implicit in our postmodern society, which is characterized by global information networks that work to project a conformist and consumerist view of the body and, at the same time, testifies to the different perceptions of the body by heterogeneous ethnic groups and peoples. The recent information revolution has forced us once again to question the relationship between the body and the machine. If it is true that the continuous bombardment of television images of mutilated and cut-up bodies has, so to speak, dematerialized them, on the other hand, the corporeality of the body comes obsessively back, as mentioned earlier, in the tribal rites that young people in the big metropolises impress on themselves.

Longino and Powell (2004, 177) further suggest that the aging body has a negative representation by cartoon fiction:

> Cartoonists tend to include deep lines on the face and loose skin beneath the chin, loss of or grey hair, a shorter distance between the nose and chin (if false teeth have been removed), glasses, liver spots on the hands, bowed legs and stooped backs. And, of course, there are the appropriate appendages and related signifiers, such as "walking canes," "walkers" or "wheel chairs." (Powell and Longino 2002)

At the other extreme, there are positive representations of aging via, for example, fictional characters from the J. R. Tolkien's *Lord of the Rings* that epitomize an agelessness, immortality, and wisdom in the role of wizardry. Nevertheless, the issue of gender and the body is crucial to understand the full complexity of aging in contemporary society.

THE GENDERED AGING BODY

Although we have analyzed modernist theoretical movements of functionalism, political economy of old age, and feminist gerontology, they ignore a postmodern understanding of aging identity, the body, cultural representations of aging, and gendered images of aging. The "gendered body" itself is a discursive site in which power is produced, acted upon, engaged with, and received. These aspects of power allow spaces for resistance to emerge, enabling power to be positive and at the same time negative. The experiences and knowledge of life before, in the celebrated young body and in the life threads of familial responsibilities and motherhood or fatherhood, can enable or disable the individual for success on the aging platform.

Theoretical arguments on gender sometimes fall prey to the philosophical error of essentialism— the appeal to metanarratives that claim to capture universal processes underlying essential differences between men and women and are insensitive to local knowledge and diversity (Harper 1997). Rather, the body is like a hinge, a pivot point, between two realities. Grosz (1994) asserts that the body is neither, while being both. Some of these binary categories are inside/outside, subject/object, and active/passive. It is not that older women are one way and older men the opposite. Bodies, whether men or women, are both ways. It is primarily their relationship to power that makes them different.

Women's stories are often about their relationship to their bodies; men's are not. Women "use" their bodies as an asset to accomplish their goals more than men do. Therefore, according to Shilling (1993), they are more likely than men to develop their bodies as objects of perception for others. The downside of this conscious embodiment of women is that as they age, they tend to lose a key asset, and thus come to think of themselves, and to be thought of, as invisible. If beauty and sexual allure are perishable values, men's power is embedded in status and wealth, more enduring values that tend to increase, not diminish, with age. The impact of the diminished assets of female identity is undeniable. Angie Dickenson, a sixty-eight-year-old American actress, reflecting on her experience of female embodiment and aging, put it well in an interview in a popular magazine:

> I'm surprised by every photograph I see of myself, because I don't look like I used to. I am not shocked anymore, just disappointed. I did look pretty good. I was all heart and sexiness, and that came from within. I had beautiful eyes, and unfortunately in trying to help them, I practically destroyed them with plastic surgery. I wish I looked now how I looked before, when I was young. (*Life* 2000, quoted in Longino and Powell 2004, 112)

Oberg and Tornstam (1999) found no evidence for the notion that women become more discontented with their bodies as they grow older, as compared with men. When asked to agree or disagree with the statement "I am satisfied with my body," about 80 percent of men agreed, regardless of their age. Only about two-thirds of young women agreed. But women in a successively older decade tended to agree more with the statement until there was essentially no difference between men and women after age sixty-five. It is younger women, not the older ones, who are the most dissatisfied.

The "body" within modernist theories of social gerontology pays insufficient attention to the ways in which gendered bodies have always enjoyed varying degrees of absence or presence in old age—in the guise of "female corporeality" and "male embodiment" (Gittens 1997). Indeed, there are discursive strategies whereby "the body" and "the social" are dissociated in the first place. In this framework, woman is saturated with, while man is divested of, corporeality. Older women have higher rates of chronic illnesses than do men, and their bodies outlast those of men. In clinical settings old women outnumber old men in nearly all waiting rooms. Yet the woman is divested while the man is invested with "the social," implying that knowledge is "gendered" and is male. The absent women in social gerontology were the women in the body excluded from the social. It is male bodies that animate the social—they appear for a fleeting moment, only to disappear immediately, in the space between "corporeality" and "sociality." Thus, it is not simply a case of recuperating bodies into the social, but of excavating the gendered discourses whereby *gendered* bodies were differently inscribed into and out of the social in the first place. The crucial point here is not the more familiar story of her saturation with corporeality but the less familiar one of what happened to *his* body. As a needed qualification, Harper (1997, 169), reminds us that because women are always embodied and men are not, "men become embodied as they age . . . through the experience of the experiential and constructed body." So the gap between women and men may narrow, in some ways, as they age.

Indeed, feminist social theorists beyond macro-based "feminist gerontology" have underlined the limits of Cartesian thought, which considered the subject as disembodied and, above all, asexual (Braidotti 1994). In the representation of the female body, the dichotomy between body and mind has been used to emphasize sexual difference. On the one hand, we have masculinity, which is defined in relation to the mind and the *logos*, while the feminine is defined in relation to the body and its procreative functions—an essentialist construction, par excellence (Twigg 2000). As Adrienne Rich reminds us, women have had to deconstruct the patriarchal stereotype that links the female body with its procreative function: "I am really asking whether women cannot begin, at last, to think through the body, to connect what has been so cruelly disorganized" (1976, 184). With this incisive sentence, Rich stresses that women have to overcome the damning dichotomy between soul and body, in order to reappropriate their bodies and to create a female subject, in which the two entities are complementary. Women often find themselves defined as "the other" (the residual category) over against men, just as black people do against white people and gay people do against heterosexual people (Harper 1997). As Harper (1997) points out, they are the ones in the shadows, not in the positions of power; the defined, not the definers. For example, as we discussed earlier, contemporary cultural representations of aging focus on the body because this provides the clearest evidence of the historical inequality between gender differentiation: the body of women is inscribed with oppressive ideological mystifications (Friedan 1993; Sontag 1991). Western literature and iconography are full of anthropomorphic discursive representations of old age as a woman with "grey hair," "withered," "faded," "pale and wan face," "foul and obscene" (Friedan 1993).

From this discussion, it would seem that the aging body is yet another mode of embodied subjectivity for gerontologists to unravel. The reterritorialization of the aging body by society, and paradigmatically by social gerontology, is a strategy that parallels the denial of wider social theory within the main traditions of social gerontology (Bengston, Burgess, and Parrot 1997). We have suggested that the concept of the "body" itself may take on particular sets of meanings for older people, both men and women, whose subjectivity of identity formation may conflict or legitimize cultural representations of aging.

The notion of "intertextuality" can be used as it is a mechanism by which the social world is fabricated, and this explains why cultural ideologies continually perpetuate perceptions of aging and gender. Postmodern perspectives can facilitate an understanding of how older people can intertextually reconstruct cultural narratives to explain their representations of identity and self-identity. Such a strategy involves a challenge to the homogeneity of the social category "elderly" as an embodiment of the "time's up" medical narrative. When the issue of social identity in later life is analyzed, Foucault's (1977) contention seems powerful in articulating that there has been a growth in the localities of power and knowledge that seek to inscribe physical and social bodies with discourses of normality and self-government. In the search for a stable identity not dominated by both professional and cultural discourses of power, older people must "achieve" it through "ontological reflexivity" (Giddens 1991). Accordingly, the self-identity needs to be consciously constructed and maintained. The aging self has a new existential pathway to follow, stepping outside dominant discourses of medical and patriarchal reason, to include a process of safety, self-exploration, self-struggle, and self-discovery (Powell and Longino 2002).

Contrary to Eurocentric philosophical traditions, feminist philosophical studies have emphasized that the body is a symbolic construct, located in a specific historical and cultural context: in other words its conceptualization can no longer ignore the close nexus between sex, class, and "race" (Blaikie 1999; Twigg 2000). Further, a significant issue for the articulation of aging with gender to further understand the "body" is represented by the theories of Foucault (1977) and Sontag (1991), which show the extent to which institutional medicine objectifies the "sick" body, once it has been *biomedicalized* (Powell 2001f). Foucault (1977) claims that medical practices produce the "soul" of the individual by disciplining the body and corporealizing medical spaces. Indeed, the success of modernity's domination over efficient bodies in industry, docile bodies in prisons, patient bodies in clinical research, and regimented bodies in schools and residential centers attest to Foucault's thesis that the human body is a highly adaptable terminus for the circulation of power relations (Powell and Biggs 2001; Armstrong 1983).

We have illuminated some of the paradoxes implicit in society, characterized by the historical discourses of decline and how they are embedded in popular culture relating to aging body and gendered body. Nevertheless, the next section shows how biotechnology networks work to project a conformist and consumerist view of the body, testifying to a different perception of the aging body by machine modification, a movement away from "expert" discourse to a new language based on "consumer identity" and "subjectivity" (Haraway 1991; Gilleard and Higgs 2000).

BIOTECHNOLOGY AND THE BODY: REINVENTING AGING?

The recent information revolution has forced us once again to question the relationship between the body and the machine. If it is true that the continuous bombardment of television images of mutilated and cut-up bodies has, so to speak, dematerialized them, on the other hand, the corporeality of the body comes obsessively back (Powell and Longino 2002; Longino and Powell 2004). However, computer communication has done away with bodily presence, and the new technologies make us see the machine as an extension of our bodies (Haraway 1991). The questions posed by this revolution in the dissemination of information are difficult to answer. It is no longer a question of emphasizing, in prophetic and apocalyptic tones, the end of Humanism but rather of understanding *how* and *to what extent* technology and science can help us to change, since technology is ultimately inextricable from our aging body, becoming an apparatus which is at the same time material and symbolic. The *cyborg,* a fusion between machine and organic body, opens up an immense universe of possibility: nowadays, we no longer speak of organic bodies but of transorganic bodies, *post-human bodies* and *bodies in the net* (Haraway 1991; Longino and Powell 2004).

These diverse forms of bodily form hold out the promise of "utopian bodies," a movement away from static medical constrainment and objectification to much more self-subjectification practices (Morris 1998; Powell and Biggs 2004). Indeed, Haraway's (1991) original reference to cyborgic fusion of biological and machine entities has been enthusiastically taken up by postmodern gerontology. The list of biotechnologies available extends beyond traditional prosthesis to include virtual identities created by and reflected in the growing number of "silver surfers" using the Internet as a free-floating form of identity management. Thus Featherstone and Wernick (1995, 3) claim that it is now possible to reconstruct "the body itself" as biomedical and information technologies make available "the capacity to alter not just the meaning, but the very material infrastructure of the body. Bodies can be re-shaped, remade, fused with machines, empowered through technological devices and extensions."

The increasing popularization of such key terms for reinvented bodies as "machine bodies" implies an effect of producing an intrasubjective consciousness, and a conspicuousness of behavior, either for bodily change or against it. Moral action, whether it is individual or collective, involves the self knowing the self, a process of self-formation as an *ethical* aging subject (Powell and Biggs 2004). Self-responsibility, when passed through the notion of the "sick body," becomes a covert form of moral judgment upon which decisions to supply or deny often expensive forms of biotechnology can be made (Powell and Biggs 2004). Indeed, one is unwell because one is unhealthy and one is unhealthy because the proper steps of self-care had not been taken in the past. So why should others have to provide scarce resources to make good this moral turpitude? Such an attitude to the healthy body presents moral decisions on the supply and demand for services in the "neutral" language of technomedical science (Powell and Biggs 2004). However, the outcome is that the prudent do not need it, while the imprudent do not deserve it. Any allusion here to economic planning and to pension policy is more than passing, for in both cases it is the resource-rich who can afford, but may rarely need, such technology, whereas the resource-poor cannot afford it (Moody 1998; Phillipson 1998). For example, biotechnology can sell as "truth" a dream of "not growing old" to older people (Powell and Biggs 2004). However, it is the self-experience of aging subjects that can refute, deny, and accept the "truth" claims of biotechnology (Rose 1996). In the case of lifestyles of the aging, the active adoption of particular consumer practices such as uses of biotechnology contributes to a narrative that is both compensatory and "ageless" in its construction of self (Biggs and Powell 2001). The aging body culturally represents the best hiding place for internal illnesses that remained inconspicuous until the advent of biotechnologies (Frank 1996). Subjective relations to the self will be affected to the extent that biotechnologies confront older people with the proposition that this subjective truth—the truth of their relation to themselves and to others—may be revealed by their "aging bodies." If this is legitimate, we may anticipate through "biology and culture" (Morris 1998) the problematic of illnesses associated with aging rejoining the sphere of bioethics through the back door. "Illness" and "body repair" as problematized by biotechnology will again belong to the strategic margin that older people embody as subjects of purposeful action.

There are obvious tensions between the biotechnological commodification of old age. It is through constructing and transgressing the aging body, by subverting the "stigma" surrounding later life (Powell and Biggs 2000), and thus redefining physical capital (May 1996) that many old bodies resisted the fixed images of old age. Moreover, within this discursive space of biotechnology the construction of the aging body allows elders to become their own significant other, to challenge the gaze of others and to "be for themselves." Their reconstructed bodies, therefore, become sites of empowerment whether they collude or resist ageist stereotypes.

CONCLUSION

This chapter has drawn insights from postmodernism, which provides compelling questions of how we interpret, problematize, and understand the body as dancing in-between *subject/object*. Hence, the chapter has demonstrated how the body is not separate from the body subject (May 1996) but is intertwined. Arthur Frank (1991, 1996) argues that, simultaneously, the embodied agent becomes a producer of society while at the same time it is society that creates the embodied agent.

It is by reimagining the boundaries of the body that we can begin to understand how the gaze inscribes itself unintelligibly on the aging body. The argument that has been presented here demonstrates an understanding of the body as both lived through and as constructed. The study of the body in gerontological literature needs to engage with the real materiality of bodies and at the same time understand the ways in which bodies are performed, represented, and positioned.

Central to this discussion is how the inscription of aging, popular culture, gender, and biotechnology are placed on and work in tandem with the rhythms of the body. The body is constantly operating within fields of temporality, in which mobile networks of relations produce and transmit power/knowledge to the object vis-à-vis subject (Butler 2000). Thus the body operates within fields of power and within the realm of signs. It has been argued that time and identity in society consist of a multiplicity of discursive elements that come into play at various times, thus existing in "different and even contradictory discourses" (Foucault 1982, 100–102). The body is a "visage," a collection of signs to be interpreted. It becomes a façade (cf. Biggs 1993), which at the same time both conceals and expresses the inner being. It is by centralizing the historical development of the body in social theory that one can illustrate and interrogate how the architecture of the ageist discourse recodes their now "profaned" bodies. Constructing some bodies as marginal and excluding them from mainstream representations defines boundaries and gives legitimacy to society's claims of what is a "natural" for a body to look.

The body is a dynamic, nebulous form, and always in the process of becoming. The contours of the body outline a visible but transitional object (Featherstone and Wernick 1995). But, as Powell and Longino (2001) argue, there is no surety of what the body is. What one can argue from discussion of the body is that it becomes the threshold through which the subject's lived experience of the world is incorporated and interpolated and, as such, can never be purely understood. The aging body is a "transitional entity"; power is produced, generated, and negotiated in terms of the inscriptions placed on the aging body in micro and local domains.

Indeed, by taking a localized approach, postmodern gerontology has been more adaptable than any "grand narrative" to address issues of power and oppression (Seidman 1994 207). By focusing on the aging body and how culture impinges on its subject formation, postmodern gerontology goes beyond fixed classifications of modern ideas deriving from biomedical sciences as well as grand narratives of macrotheories of aging (Longino and Powell 2004; Powell 2001c). This is a view consolidated by Bauman (2001), who points to the way that society has become increasingly individualized. All individual lives are affected by localized conditions and narratives, and what is needed is an analysis of the extent to which the individual is governed by external conditions in terms of their life choices (Bauman 2001, 6–7). Bauman argued that postmodern culture is effectively a competitive market, trading in "life meanings" (Bauman 2001, 4), and this can be linked to Lyotard's suggestion that knowledge has become the product of different "specialisms" to be bought and sold for profit (Lyotard 1984, 5). For example, the fragmentation of the aging body has become a commodifiable social space through which biotechnologies can offer body reconstruction in consumer-led Western society through machine extensions to the body (Powell and Longino 2002).

Similarly, Frederic Jameson (1991) understood postmodernism as an extension of the "logic of late capitalism." Jameson argued that globalization and multinational capitalism had resulted in mass consumerism and the *total* commodification of culture, in which "images, styles and representations . . . are the products themselves" (Connor 1989, 46). However, Stuart Hall argues that the postmodern idea of cultural homogenization is too simplistic (Hall 1992, 304). He suggests that in a restructuring of social theory we should acknowledge how the global and the local articulate and recognize that globalization is unevenly distributed and is also a Western phenomenon indicative of the unequal power relations between the "west and the rest." Estes, Biggs, and Phillipson (2003) consolidate this by suggesting that Occidental globalization affects the poverty status of older people universally.

Nevertheless, the great strength of postmodernism is to dissect *fixed* discourses of modernity and reveal alternative cultural processes that impinge on both epistemic and ontologically flexible narratives pertaining to the human body. As Seidman states, modernist social theory was focused on neat divisions, hierarchies, and foundational premises, and the aim of sociologists was to find universalisms (Seidman 1994, 347).

Postmodernism, on other hand, was to look at subject formation re-garding the body as it has been overlooked by macromodernist theories. Whereas postmodernists would question the notion of truth and focus on intrasubjective dimensions of bodily performance, the conceptual "tool kit" Foucault has added allows wider insights to power relation-ships between and through subjects/objects of knowledge and profes-sional experts.

Indeed, the critical relationship of aging to society and interaction in power relationships has found expression in writings of Foucault. Fou-cault is not a postmodernist (Smart 1993) but his work has been bound up with it because of Foucault's (1977) own questioning of the "truth" status of epistemological knowledge through historical medical and criminal discourses. His work shifts to the interplay of self-subjectification prac-tices grounded in power/knowledge (Foucault 1977), technologies of self (1978) and governmentality (1978) at microphysical levels of society that operate between social actors such as doctor and patient, teacher and pupil, prison officer and prisoner, and health professional and older per-son as "client." The next chapter explores the "Foucault effect" on geron-tological theorizing and its relevance to how power relations play out in interactions of professional welfare experts with older people by analysis of "discourse," "power/knowledge," "technologies of self," and "govern-mentality."

5

The "Foucault Effect" and Aging

Relations of Power, Surveillance, and Governmentality

> Add Foucault and stir. . . .
>
> —Shumway 1989, 5

> The theories Foucault devised are not intended as permanent structures, enduring in virtue of their universal truth. They are temporary scaffoldings, erected for a specific purpose, which Foucault is happy to abandon to [whoever] might find them useful.
>
> —Gutting 1994, 16)

INTRODUCTION

The subject matter of this chapter is the development of an understanding of aging and professional power over the past fifty years, using examples drawn from social welfare and old age, through developing the theories and philosophies derived from the French social theorist, Michel Foucault. Whereas chapter 4 focused on postmodernism and the body in Western culture, this chapter consolidates analysis of the aging body, to explore the interrelationship between discourse, professional power, and intersubjectivity. Foucault's concepts and ideas have become significantly influential in a variety of social science disciplines. At the same time they can be puzzling for those wishing to understand their implications for analyzing professional power and aging. Foucault was a "masked philosopher" who deliberately sought to avoid being aligned with any particular school of thought: "It is true that I prefer not to identify myself, and that I'm amused by the diversity of the ways I've been judged and classified" (1997, 113). For example, David Garland (1985) claims that Foucault has had a "huge impression" on criminological studies and allowed the discipline to develop a new theoretical language. Foucault is yet to have the same effect on social gerontology. Unfortunately, Foucault said little about aging, and one can only speculate as to the ingenuity of his insights on the subject had he lived into old age himself (Katz 1996).

Michel Foucault's scholarly work has been acclaimed as "the most important event in thought of our century" (Veyne 1980, 44). Throughout his work, Foucault has attempted to develop perspectives on psychiatry, medicine, punishment, and criminology.

Indeed, Foucault's diverse range of theoretical works highlights two significant contexts in the analyses of aging. The first is to assert the relevance of discipline and punishment and madness and medicine to both the representations and experiences of older people. The introduction of the "expert gaze" in health and medical professions allows the space for exploration of discourses and impingement of stereotypical "subjects" of knowledge such as the "mentally ill," "criminals," and also the "elderly" as they are constructed through disciplinary techniques.

Secondly, Foucault's (1980) discursive analytical "tools" enable us to analyze both the authoritative discourses embodied in public policies and professional practices within society, in particular the power relations between professional workers and older people (Powell and Biggs 2000). Foucault's scholarly works (1967, 1976, 1977) have relevance to "old age" in the respect that social practices describe patterns of "normalization" in a political landscape dominated by consumer culture. It will be shown that these practices, which are evaluated by "experts" such as "care managers" who problematize "the elderly" (Powell and Biggs 2000) via a process of "assessment" for social and health services in contemporary society, are the center of Foucault's (1977) analysis of "panoptic technology" in "surveying" and managing "elderly" clients. Before we assess the relevance of these gerontological issues, we need to situate the work of Foucault as a contextual backdrop to understanding old age and professional power.

CONTEXTUAL BACKDROP OF
FOUCAULT'S EARLY STRUCTURALISM

The structuralist approach saw the world from a completely opposing viewpoint, their world being "pre-structured" and we, as humans, structured in it. Structuralists take one step back in looking at how the world is organized to influence peoples' self-understanding, from a sense of cultural relation and personal reference or identity within particular social conformities (Powell and Wahidin 2003). As Dreyfus and Rabinow (1983, 8) have asserted: "structuralism attempts to dispense with both meaning and the subject by finding objective laws which govern all human activity."

In opposition to this position, the general foundation of hermeneutics releases the phenomenologists' attempt to understand man as a "meaning-giving subject," but attempts to preserve meaning by locating it in the social practices and literary texts that authors produce. A product of his time, Foucault during the 1960s argued against an entire philosophical and political structure where two main streams of thought existed in fundamental Marxism and psychoanalysis. The problem with psychoanalysis was that it attempted to explain everything from one theory or viewpoint, that being via "infantile sexualism." This speculative individualist reductionism was inadequate in explaining the complexities of various local group uprisings within society during those times. It was particularly inadequate to explain the mentality of the masses of people who united as one individualized group to revolt against existing structures that had been suppressing both the individual's sense of "self" and the distinct groups that they identified with. Foucault is often seen as a structuralist, along with Barthes, Althusser, and Levi-Strauss (May 1996). In reply to questions that sought to make such parallels, he was consistent: "I am obliged to repeat it continually. I have never used any of the concepts which can be considered characteristic of structuralism" (Foucault, quoted in May 1996, 88). Perhaps the best way to view this is by examining his idea of historical "events." He refuses to see events as symptomatic of deeper social structures and focuses upon what seems to be marginal as indicative of relations of power. Events thereby differ in their capacity to produce effects. The following quote helps us see how this can be applied to gerontological analysis:

> The problem is at once to distinguish among events, to differentiate the networks and levels to which they belong, and to reconstitute the lines along

which they are connected and engender one another. From this follows a refusal of analyses couched in terms of the symbolic field or the domain of signifying structures, and a recourse to analyses in terms of the genealogy of relations of force, strategic development, and tactics. Here I believe one's point
of reference should not be to the great model of language (langue) and signs,
but to that of war and battle. (Foucault 1980, 114)

Structuralism can be seen as an important asset to the development of
social research, and particularly for social gerontology in terms of the promotion of introspection on their life-course by the elderly "subjects of
study" and reflections by researchers, policy makers, and the general public on the problematization of "old age" within society and government. It
is also important for its discourses into the radical empowerment of older
citizens in therapeutic programs to resist suppressive regulatory norms
imposed and induced by institutionalized care. Lastly, structuralism provides historical mapping of the changes in our understandings of concepts over time, or lack thereof, within the systems of health and aged
care, through analysis of authoritative writings such as policy documents.
For instance, the concept of "health" and how we legislate for health has
changed considerably since the Poor Law Reform Act of 1834 in Great
Britain (Phillipson 1982). This movement acts as a significant benchmark
for the origins of institutionalized aged care, which began with authoritative control in managing the masses of vagrants, homeless, and the poor,
many of whom were older people (Katz 1996, 55).

Foucault's early works on *Madness and Civilization* and *The Birth of the
Clinic* focused on the analysis of historically situated systems of institutions
and discursive practices—which were distinguished from the "speech acts"
of everyday life. Foucault did not look at individual's narratives but was interested only in what Dreyfus and Rabinow (1983, xxiv) called "serious
speech acts," which were what experts perform when they are speaking as
experts about a given issue within a discipline of thought or practice such
as law or medicine. Furthermore, Foucault's restriction of these analyses to
the human sciences introduced new methods to critique the emergence of
pseudoscientific tools of analysis within the study of human beings, such as
psychoanalysis and sociology, which, with their speculative, introspective,
and retrospective techniques in understanding human behavior, were considered as "dubious" disciplines (Wahidin and Powell 2001, 2003).

In *The Archaeology of Knowledge* (1972) Foucault introduced his "archaeological method" whereby the interrelations between the artifacts of

study, that is, the people involved, are analyzed for insights into the "power relationships" existing within the structure of these relationships and how the social institutions in which these particular structures existed influenced the discursive practices.

Like Thomas Kuhn's paradigmatic shifts, the Foucauldian discursive practices appear antistructuralist in that there are structures that explain a discourse, such as the fundamental acceptance of the state as the controller of power, which influences and exerts power upon groups and society in general. Foucault's work is beyond structuralism and hermeneutics and is useful in historically situating gerontology within a context of ordering and systematizing practices characteristic of the disciplinary technologies. His interest in the social effects rather than the implicit meaning of banal practices leaves hermeneutic concerns behind.

Foucault's way of reading history proves powerful in understanding the emergence of gerontology in that he manages to both criticize and utilize "phenomenology, hermeneutics and structuralism" (Smart 1993), thus enabling one to explain how the study of elderly people as subjects and objects has had such centrality in both history and culture. Foucault's refusal to be characterized in particular ways may be interpreted as an intentional political strategy central to his overall philosophy. He rejects any allusion to certainty in social and political life and holds that there is no universal understanding beyond history—placing him at odds with currents in Marxism, as well as rationalist thought in general. That noted, we can find imperatives that receive differing degrees of emphasis throughout his work, one of which is "to discover the relations of specific scientific disciplines and particular social practices" (Rabinow 1984, 4). He has engendered an awareness that disciplines, institutions, and social practices operate according to logics that are at variance with the humanist visions that are assumed to be culturally embedded (Powell and Biggs 2000).

The analytical audaciousness of Foucault's approach can be applied to Foucauldian aspects of aging but such forms of knowledge base remains relatively small in social gerontology (Katz 1996).

FOUCAULDIAN GERONTOLOGY

Only a tiny handful of international gerontologists have used Foucault's work to shatter taken-for-granted assumptions centered on aging. In

Canada, Stephen Katz's (1996) *Disciplining Old Age: The Formation of Gerontological Knowledge* is a landmark via Foucauldian analysis of aging. This work is a theoretically rigorous analysis of the emergence of gerontology as a discipline from the study of old age. Katz's explorations into the social, political, organizational, and epistemological frameworks involved in the "gerontological web" had articulately demonstrated their influence in the negative characterizations of the elderly as a distinct kind of population. Katz's adept incorporation of Foucauldian theories into an analysis of gerontology showed how the discipline emerged through discourses from the various authoritative powers or "experts" in the health and academic professions, via their writings or "master narratives," associations, funding organizations, and schools of thought. Katz (1996) has identified that aging is not a static process and for this reason cannot be singularly analyzed via any particular discipline. By use of Foucault's work, Katz (1996) demonstrates that the challenge to "age disciplines" impinges upon the "power/knowledge" axis. Crucially, such an axis permeates all formal and informal discourses, their language, logic, forms of domination and classification, measurement techniques and empiricism as essential elements in the technology of discipline and the process of normalization. "Professionals" such as gerontologists and geriatricians are key interventionists in societal relations and, in the management of social arrangements, wield a daunting power to classify, with consequences for the reproduction of knowledge about aging and simultaneous maintenance of power relations (Powell 1998). According to Powell (1998) Katz's work demonstrates that the challenges to mainstream "age disciplines" have adopted the agendas of these traditions, taking their historical and contemporary agendas as legitimate points of departure. While starting with "knowledge as it stands," that which is "known," Katz reconstructs such knowledge at the interpersonal level of "agency."

In the United Kingdom, Tulle-Winton (1999) has looked at the notion of the body and its relationship to Foucauldian theories of embodiment. Powell has applied the "Foucauldian gaze" to understanding the "ageing body" (2001) and governmentality and social policy (2001). The works of Powell and Biggs (2000) and Biggs and Powell (2000, 2001) have developed Foucauldian approaches relating to "medical power and social welfare" (Powell and Biggs 2000), "care management and elder abuse" (Biggs and Powell 2000), and genealogies of professional power and aging

(Biggs and Powell 2001). In addition, Powell and Cook (2000, 2001) have developed perspectives on governmentality and "superaging" in China. Coupled with this, Wahidin and Powell (2001) have used Foucauldian narratives to examine "institutional abuse" in special hospitals Wahidin and Powell 2001). May (1996) has explored nursing's development of holistic care with older people as contributing to the rise and consolidation of disciplinary power of the nurse over the older patient through "therapeutic surveillance."

Biggs and Powell (2001) have described studies that adopt Foucault's conceptual insights as exploring "the differential ways in which bodies are regulated, understood and constructed." Estes, Biggs, and Phillipson (2003) locate a progressive movement toward the construction of the "whole person" as the object of care "gazes" and through a change toward risk-oriented practice. Powell (2001) in his Foucauldian analysis of aging identified how professional practices used to elicit information and profiles about aging populations came to be linked to biomedical techniques and practices used at the individual level in constructing the object of scientific study. Thus statistical data about the nature of older people's health consolidated the biomedical gaze on visual inspection of older people's bodies and minds. The object of study in the nexus of "microphysics of power" is a capillary form of power reaching to the very minutia of detailed profiling of an individual person and profiles of aging populations. Through history, the knowledge base of biomedical practice has shifted to include survey data about social circumstances and beliefs and their effects on care. Professional power emphasized supporting and negotiating strategies in communication with patients in order to alter and shape behavior. What Powell (2001a) is highlighting is that the object of biomedicine as being reconstructed as both object and subject.

Fundamentally, the use of a "Foucauldian" approach in social gerontology is a novel way of interpreting and problematizing knowledge systems. It provides new questions, objects of inquiry, and flexible epistemological and ontological dimensions of gerontological analysis. While retaining a concern with the dynamics of power and knowledge, embedded within and (re)produced by social policy, a Foucauldian approach shifts attention away from a sole analysis of the state, the logic of capital, or patterns of material inequality. Power remains a concept central to any Foucauldian understanding of the social processes and institutional practices but in novel and varying ways.

The effect of this has been to call into question—draw into a field of interrogation—the categories and assumptions standing at the heart of social gerontology, understood here as both a disciplinary field of knowledge and as a practice that focuses on social policy and aging. In raising the question of "knowledge" as a socially constituted category through which "power" is manifested and deployed, a Foucauldian approach can destabilize the notion of a "universal" human subject whose needs can be known through the application of bureaucratic procedures, that is, the subject who is the target of professional power (Katz 1996). This means that the ontological status of the gerontological "subject" becomes open not only to deconstructive scrutiny but also to epistemological discourses by which this subject is categorized and classified.

It can be argued that it is through "historical investigation" that scholars can understand the present which takes aim at understanding Foucault's potential use of methods to understanding social formations relevant to adult aging. If we use "historical inquiry" we should "use it, to deform it, to make it groan and protest" (Foucault 1980, 54). Historical critique should be used to shatter taken-for-granted biomedical assumptions surrounding aging. But Powell and Biggs (2001, 10) warn that this focus: "on medicalization . . . has tended to obscure another . . . discourse on aging . . . the association between old age and social welfare."

As we discussed earlier, gerontology is also the study of social welfare and social policy focused on aging (Biggs 1999). Social policy for older people in "neoliberal" capitalist societies is complex and multifaceted. Neoliberalism considers that a welfare society must reflect only the interplay of social and political structures forged out of self-responsibility and consumerism (Powell 2001c). Older people derive their "care," individually and collectively, from a range of policies, institutions, and sites, so that the organization of care involves markets, families, and state and care institutions. Responsibility for the organization of "care-based" social policy has historically been the social work profession or the contemporary care management institution (Powell 2001d).

Medical discourses and neoliberal norms of the positioning of older people are not only about the therapeutic nature of the "health and care" duality, drawn from medical sciences, but also, if not more, about "management enforcers" (Biggs 1999) of competition, quality, inspection, and customer demand.

These definitions of analytical frameworks on aging have significant implications for how "aging" is understood, both as a discipline of study and as a social process: as a discipline in interrogating how knowledge in modernity has been organized and legitimated and as a social process in terms of complex interactions between recent social policy shifts, professional experts, and older people. In combination, these definitions refer to the discourses, perceptions, sites, and practices that are conditions of possibility for the emergence of gerontological knowledge. Engaging with these possibilities for knowledge construction requires a methodological means and gerontological definitional examples drawn from medical power and their antecedent relationship to the positioning of older people as "declining" subjects/objects.

The effects of the decline analogy can be most clearly seen in the dominance of medico-technical solutions to the problems that aging is thought to pose. This, according to Katz (1996), has led to a significant skewing of gerontological theorizing and research toward geriatric medicine, as well as the relative failure of more broadly based social and life-course approaches to change thinking about old age.

Conversely, a preoccupation with the medical challenges presented by aging, underpinned by privatized and insurance-driven health provisions, has resulted in what Foucault (1973) may have observed as an expansion of the medical "gaze" into wider areas of social policy. The medical gaze refers here to discourses, languages, and ways of seeing that shape the understanding of aging into questions that center on, and increase the power of, the health professions and restrict or delegitimize other possibilities. A consequence is that areas of policy that may at first seem tangential to the medical project come to be reflected in its particular distorting mirror.

The influence of the medical gaze can be seen in the policy debates of the late 1980s and early 1990s concerning disadvantaged groups, over a shrinking public purse and fears of a breakdown of an intergenerational social contract, considered to be a foundation of postwar welfare policy (Phillipson 1998). The impact of medicalized notions of aging and its construction as a threat to other sections of the population can also be seen in Harry R. Moody's (1998) critique of bioethics and aging and the rationing of Medicare coverage in American welfare policy. Medical care has come to colonize notions of old age and reinforce ageist prejudices to the extent that infirmity has come to stand for the process of aging itself and medicine its potential, yet prohibitively expensive, savior.

Foucault's (1967, 1972) early works impinge on how "epistemic" discourses *problematized* human subjectivity. His later work is much more grounded in the interplay of power and knowledge, governmentality, and technologies of self. If we take summaries of both his early and later works, in turn, we can see the relevance of his overall *oeuvre* to theorizing professional power and aging. Foucault (1977) was principally interested in how particular forms of knowledge came into existence and the social conditions that made this possible. The next section draws from this and sketches the main developments of expert discourses by digging into the past in order to explain present social practices.

The "Expert" Gaze and Discourse of Dependency

Foucault's concern in his earlier structuralist work (1967, 1972) was to show that the epistemological and "truth" status of medical and scientific knowledge derives from the field in which it, as a discourse, is employed, and not from a hermeneutic interpretation of the discoursing subjects' thoughts. A discourse is a set of ideas, practices, and beliefs that coalesce to produce an overarching picture of society. He deliberately subordinated the individual subjects' will to the construction of medical and scientific discourses, as he set about exploring the relationship between such discourses and human subjectivity.

Coupled with this, the "aging body" became the site of medical and scientific practice and designated experts developed the medical gaze with which they viewed and defined human physical properties (Powell 2001a, 2001b; Powell and Biggs 2000; Biggs and Powell 2001). The construction of subjects as authorities, knowers, and speakers of knowledge, is a controversial linking of professional discourse and its dialectical interplay with the subjectivity of older people.

Indeed, the emergence of professional power in what has since come to be called modernity is also associated with transformations that took place from the nineteenth century onward. In the case of social welfare, these transformations have been associated with a series of moral panics about the family in which the state was expected to intervene (Jones 1983). Professional social work developed in this space between public and private spheres and was produced by sets of relations among the law, administration, medicine, the school, and the family. The rise and consolidation of social work was seen as a "benevolent" solution to a major problem posed to the liberal state, namely, how can the state establish the health and development of family members who are "dependent" while promoting the family as the "natural" sphere for caring for those individuals and thus not intervening in all families (Hirst 1981)? Thus, social work developed as a halfway point between individual families and the state, which would be in danger of taking responsibility for everybody's needs and hence undermining the responsibility and role of the family. This hybrid and somewhat ambivalent positioning of a new discipline meant that from its inception the social work profession has had to negotiate the boundary between public expectation and private conduct.

The traditional identity of professional social work rests on what can be identified as "modernist" foundations (Biggs and Powell 2001). While nursing and medicine have drawn heavily on technical/scientific knowledge to justify their expert status, social work has drawn, with relative degrees of success and in succeeding periods, on psychoanalysis and the social sciences. Both health and welfare have been part of a great movement for "progress" characteristic of the twentieth-century grand narrative.

As the twentieth century proceeded, the growth of social work became increasingly dependent upon its interrelationships with the welfare state, which provided its primary rationale and legitimacy. As a consequence, social work mediated not only between potentially socially excluded individuals and the state, but also between those individuals and diverse private and voluntary agencies. Further, social work as an expert profession became closely related to the development of new forms of social regulation associated with the increased complexity of modern society (Garland 1985).

Throughout the 1940s, 1950s, and 1960s, the new human sciences had as their central aim the prediction of future behavior (Ignatieff 1978), which fit well with social work's professional mission and what emerged as its chosen method: psychoanalysis (Biggs 1999). The point here is that this negative stance, coupled with the need for a discourse that both reinforced professional power and the marginal positioning of older people, found each other in the early use of psychodynamic language by social workers on both American and British sides of the Atlantic. Thus, the "caring" profession tended to draw upon psychoanalytic discourse to socially construct an image of older people as "greedy and demanding, always clamoring for material help, always complaining of unfair treatment or deprivation; this attitude shades into paranoid imagining" (Irvine 1954, 27). This psychologized view of failing independence closely parallels an economic discourse that old age constitutes a drain on resources that could be used more "productively."

Such an expert "gaze" constructs older people as both subjects and objects of knowledge and power. As Powell and Biggs (2000, 7) elaborate: "The identities of elderly people and old age have been constructed through expert discourses of 'decay' and 'deterioration' and the 'gaze' helps to intensify regulation over older people in order to normalize and provide treatment for such notions."

Techniques of surveillance are so sophisticated, argues Foucault, that "inspection functions ceaselessly. The gaze is everywhere" (1977, 195). Foucault points here to the means through which power is exercised. He places the processes of discipline, surveillance, individualization, and normalization at the center of his analysis. These processes were key elements in the genesis of public welfare agencies from the inception of the British welfare state in 1945 (Phillipson 1998). For example, social work with older people was part of a strategy that extended "control over minutiae of the conditions of life and conduct" (Cousins and Hussain 1984, 146). Within this discourse, the professional social worker became "the great advisor and expert" (Rabinow 1984, 283–84) in the utilization of medicoscientific insights in constructing services for older people.

Discourses of "dependency" formed the foundations of practice development in modernity in relation to older people. The notion of dependency was articulated in terms of policy through the state provision of care services and via social work through the practice of caregiving to older people (Bowl 1986). The aim of such policy was to deliver security to people moving into later life both through financial provision and care services.

Thus a discourse of dependency came to colonize wider perceptions of aging, and as welfarism became the place in which older people became visible to the rest of society (Powell and Biggs 2000). This position was reinforced as knowledge was collected on older populations throughout such agencies and remedies channeled through their offices. Psychoanalytic thinking, rather than an occasion for psychological liberation, became the language and the technique through which the identities of professionals and their clients were shaped.

Under particular social circumstances, discourses emerged that led to the creation of new professions that, in turn, simultaneously reinforced the discourse itself. In that process, a new type of knowledge about older people emerged, and new sites in which to grow old were created. Foucault (1967) was particularly interested in the limits and possibilities of discourses from "human sciences" because of their attempts to define human subjectivity. His attention shifts to the power of professionals because Foucault found that the conditions of possibility for "true" discourses about human subjects include complex relations between knowledge about people and systems of power. Here Foucault focuses on the techniques of power/knowledge that operate within an institution and that simultaneously create "a whole domain of knowledge and a whole type of power" (1977, 185). These domains effectively destroy the legitimacy of other, competing, discourses, just as a professional medical opinion might delegitimize voices arising from folk medicine (Freund 1988) or even informal care (Dalley 1988). As Biggs and Powell (2001, 111) warn: "If they are not careful, both professionals and users of health and welfare systems become trapped in a dance of mutually maintained positions that serves to sustain a particular view of aging and the remedies, the technologies, that can be brought to bear on it."

Subjectivity, Power/Knowledge and Professional "Practices" of Discourse

Foucault's later work on the "history of the present," was more interested in "power/knowledge" synthesis and how the subject was formed (Foucault 1977, 1978). Here, Foucault's work is on the "microphysics of power" and the interplay of power relations, dividing practices, and tactics in localistic contexts (Foucault 1977): the doctor and the patient; prison officer and prisoner; teacher and student; and care manager and older consumer (Biggs and Powell 2000; Powell 2001d).

Foucault's archaeological method is not theoretical but "genealogical." As a technique of isolating discourse objects for study, it serves to separate and defamiliarize the serious discourse of the human sciences, which in turn allows Foucault to raise the genealogical questions: "How are these discourses used? What role do they play in society?" (Dreyfus and Rabinow 1983, xxv). Foucault acquired the concept of "genealogy" from the writings of F. Nietzsche. Genealogy maintains elements of archaeology, including the analysis of statements in the archive (Foucault 1977, 1980, 1982). With genealogy Foucault (1977) added a concern with the analysis of power/knowledge, which manifests itself in the "history of the present." As Rose points out, genealogy concerns itself with disreputable origins and "unpalatable functions." For example, Biggs and Powell's (1999, 2001) genealogy of psycho-casework and care management points to the origins, functions, and practices of social work as a scientific and managerial profession that are less benevolent than official histories of professional practice pretend. As Foucault (1980, 109) found in his exploration of psychiatric power: "Couldn't the interweaving effects of power and knowledge be grasped with greater certainty in the case of a science as 'dubious' as psychiatry?"

Foucault (1977, 1978) focuses on the techniques of power that operate within an institution and which simultaneously create "a whole domain of knowledge and type of power" (Foucault 1977, 185). Biggs and Powell (2001) point out that a genealogical argument, as related to professional power, works to "[uncloak] these power relations [and] is characterised, by Foucault, to set out to examine the 'political regime of the production of truth'" (Davidson 1986, 224).

As institutions of power such as social work, newly redefined as "case management" (Powell 2002; Biggs and Powell 2001), arose, they brought into existence new clientele groups such as "consumers" who could be defined as "different" from wider age-based "population formations" based on discourses of "burden" and "dependency" (Powell 2001d). With the marketization of welfare, social work has been significantly eroded, and with it their traditional role as provider and counsellor of services for older people. Not only do new discourses provide a "swarming" of professional power/knowledge, they can also take away. At the same time, the technique of "panopticism" was incorporated into social work relationships in the twentieth century so that older people could be observed by professional power (Powell and Biggs 2000). Social service provision for older people has elements of this kind of surveillance. Supervision is hierarchical in the sense that many mature adults are accompanied by management discretionary power which embraces monitoring, assessing, and calculating older people (Powell and Biggs 2000). Social service departments need to be kept informed of their clientele's progress in order to communicate this at formal review meetings, to establish resource allocation, to service spending planning. Surveillance of older people does not stop at this point, as a network of reciprocal power relationships has been created (Powell and Biggs 2000): "[T]his network 'holds' the whole together and traverses it in its entirety with effects of power that derive from one another: supervisors, perpetually supervised" (Foucault 1977, 176–77).

Older people who require welfare services are the objects of scrutiny within Western society, but for such clients requiring financial services, the gaze reaches further. This evidences a strategic shift toward the policing of welfare and away from the postwar welfare consensus relationship to old age. Old age then became, in this period, increasingly associated with risk, both personal and structural, and at the same time was subject to a privatization of that risk and a withdrawal or rolling back of supports, previously taken as stable and enduring (Biggs and Powell 2001). It is not by chance that an increased focus on risk in social work has coincided with the decline in trust in social workers' expertise, decision-making through psychoanalytical insights, and a growing reliance on increasingly complex systems of managerialism, with older people themselves as "consumers" of services. Hence, the managerial gaze has come to rival the biomedical gaze. The power of the "case manager" as a gerontological expert has supplemented medical power.

Foucault's (1977) idea that power is a "relationship" expresses the effect that repression and productivity will occur with this control over people. A new structure then enters that promotes the possibility for a revolution in thinking or in existing policies, and also a fundamental shift in the power relations between the controller and those being controlled (Powell 2001). The implications are suitable for a critique of how aged-care institutions can appear as suppressive organizations of authoritative power upon the elderly masses in their care (Powell and Biggs 2000). The trickle-down effect of power from the apex of authority, that of the State and its policies, leaves the individual in this power relationship with very little power or sense of autonomy or individuality after being filtered through a complex hierarchy of professional and direct care staff (Clough and Hadley 1996). Institutionalized care can be seen to portray the elderly as a mass of individuals grouped together by similar socioeconomic and physical characteristics to conjure negative images of the elderly population and that of the aging process (Wahidin and Powell 2001).

At the same time, the voices of professionals become louder and older people's voices become softer in the domain of power/knowledge and the politics of social relations. Clough's (1988) study of abuse at a residential care home in England exemplified this. Many staff had neglected older residents. The abuse included neglecting to bathe residents; punishing those residents who left hot water running in bathrooms or opened windows for air; and removing blankets from residents, leading to pneumonia and subsequently many deaths. Vousden (1987, cited in Hadley and Clough 1995) claimed that professionals destroyed the positive identity of many older people in such a repressive residential regime:

> It is self evident that when elderly, often confused residents are made to eat their own faeces, are left unattended, are physically man-handled or are forced to pay money to care staff and even helped to die, there is something seriously wrong. (Vousden 1987, quoted in Clough and Hadley 1996, 55)

Hence, the power/knowledge twist of professional "carers" was detrimental to policy statements concerning "choice" and "quality of life" in residential care. Such care action was a powerful and repressive mechanism used to indent and strip the identities of residents. Biggs and Powell (2001) claim a Foucauldian approach highlights that such professions retain a powerful position in U.K. care policy, not only in terms of what they *do* but what they *say*:

> Foucault identified discourses as historically variable ways of specifying knowledge and truth. They function as sets of rules, and the exercise of these rules and discourses in programmes which specify what is or is not the case—what constitutes "old age," for example. Those who are labelled "old" are in the grip of power. This power would include that operated by professionals through institutions and face to face interactions with their patients and clients. Power is constituted in discourses and it is in discourses such as those of "social work," that power lies. (Biggs and Powell 2001, 97)

Professional power under the guise of "case management" "makes sense" as part of a discourse that displaces and reduces the financial "burden" of age on the state and onto the families of vulnerable older people (Biggs and Powell 2000). Economic privatization is accompanied by a wish to see those same older people as active consumers, making choices between services and changing services or residence if they are found wanting. There has been little consideration, however, of the financial costs, the costs to well-being, or the ability of such vulnerable groups to act in accordance within a discourse based on consumption (Biggs and Powell 2001).

While case management has proved an effective technology for transforming welfare economies, it has made little sense in terms of the preceding social work ethos of counselling and direct care (Leonard 1997). Social workers are now the risk assessors and enforcers of a mixed welfare economy, a discourse that leaves older people who use services on the contradictory and risky ground of being simultaneously consumers and potential victims (Powell 2001c). An unwillingness to increase public finance for older people had led the political administrations of presidents Clinton (1992–2000) and Bush (2000–) in the United States and that of Britiish prime minister Blair (1997–) to leave the market-welfare systems of both North America and Britain relatively untouched.

The next section introduces notions of "technologies of self" and "governmentality" and assesses their relevance to subjectification practices of older people in post-welfare societies.

RETHINKING AGING: TOWARD "TECHNOLOGIES OF SELF" AND GOVERNMENTALITY?

What has not been delineated sufficiently is Foucault's (1978) later works of "technologies of self" and "governmentality." Foucault contextualized the value of subjectivity as a pivotal mode of analysis. Subjectivity is a core idea that "goes beyond theory" (Dreyfus and Rabinow 1983) and a delineation of its ramifications for gerontological study is a useful way to "problematize" the explanatory value of a Foucauldian analysis based on "technologies of self" and governmentality.

Foucault's final works (1976, 1988) on "technologies of self" and sexuality focus on individual self-subjectification practices that challenge dominant discursive representations of social types. Here, Powell (2001e) develops this by pointing to the interplay of "resistance" and domination.

An effect of the mutually reinforcing relationship between power and knowledge that emerges from the above is to construct individuals simultaneously as subjects and as objects. First, people are seen as objects by someone else, through control and restraint. Second, people are deemed to actively subject their own identity to personal direction through processes such as conscience and mediated self-knowledge. Foucault (1988) refers to this second process as "technologies of self."

Foucault's latter works (1988) on technologies of self and sexuality focus on individual self-subjectification practices which challenge dominant discursive representations of idiographic types. Here, Powell and Biggs (2002) develop this by pointing to interplay of "resistance" with domination.

Examples of how technologies are deployed in managing old age can be found in the work of Frank (1996) on stories of illness, Katz (2000) on active aging and "busy bodies," and in Biggs's (2001) critique of contemporary social policy. In each case, macrosocial practices have become translated into particular ways of growing old that not only shape what it is to age successfully, but are also adopted by older adults, modified to fit their own life circumstances, and then fed back into wider narratives of aging well.

For Frank (1996) the personal experience of illness is mediated by biomedical procedures that shape and contribute to how the older patient recognizes his or her own process of ill health and recovery. For Katz (1999) the maxim of "activity for its own sake" as a means of managing later life not only reflects wider social values concerning work and nonwork, it also provides personal means of control and acts as grounds for resistance. Biggs (2001) argues that policy interest has changed from seeing old age as a burden to seeing it as an opportunity to promote productive aging. This reflects an attempt to shape acceptable forms of aging while encouraging older adults to self-monitor their own success at conforming to the new paradigm. A common thread throughout relies on the adoption of values and the availability of technologies that facilitate self-scrutiny and self-modification.

Powell (2002) suggests that "technologies of self" and "governmentality" are linked in understanding social relations in society. Indeed, Foucault's work (1978) on "governmentality" challenges Marxist and feminist gerontological perspectives, which claim that "state power" reproduces class differences, of which "elderly" people are "victims" with "low pension provision" (Phillipson 1982), while "gender" differences in care provision epitomize a "patriarchal" state (Arber and Ginn 1995). The existing theoretical literature on governmentality refers to Foucault and his concept of a new style of governance in modernity. It is characterized by the "ensemble formed by the institutions, procedures, analyses and reflections, the calculations and tactics that allow the exercises of this very specific albeit complex form of power" (Foucault 1978, quoted in Burchell et al. 1991, 102). According to Foucault (1978, quoted in Burchell et al. 1991) governmentality comprises three tiers: it is the result of transformations within the modern state; it is a tendency to institutionalize a particular form of power, and it is the "en-semble formed by institutions, procedures, analyses and reflections . . . calculations and tactics" (102–3) that enable the exercise of power directed toward the regulation of an (aging) population using various professional apparatuses of security.

For Foucault (1978) government is concerned with the "conduct of conduct," and neoliberal government is especially concerned with inculcating a new set of values and objectives oriented toward incorporating individual older people as both players and partners in a marketized social system. In such a regime older people are exhorted, indeed expected, to become entrepreneurs in all spheres and to accept responsibility for the management of risk (Beck 1992); older people then govern themselves.

Indeed, on a societal level some authors interpret risk as a new meta-narrative strongly linked to the neoliberal projects of government (Powell 2001a). Coupled with this, Rose and Miller argue, we must investigate political rationalities and technologies of government, "the complex of mundane programmes, calculations, techniques, apparatuses, documents and procedures through which authorities seek to embody and give effect to governmental ambitions" (1992, 175). Technologies of government consist of complex devices and practices through which social groups such as care professionals attempt to operationalize, following Rose and Miller, their program of tailoring knowledge for older people (Powell 2001a). Such technologies, Rose and Miller (1992) suggest, articulate and deploy political rationalities and thereby enable action-at-a-distance.

While there is increasing dependence on professional expertise, there is also a drive to make, for example, older people active participants in their own rule via empowerment (Biggs 1999). One of the ways of facilitating both is the representation of issues as nonpolitical, so that expert knowledge becomes dominant in "rendering the complexities of modern social and economic life knowable, practicable and amenable to governing" (Johnson 1995, 23).

Furthermore, there is a multiplication of sources and types of authority and a proliferation of social actors in social policy spaces, so that "so many of those who are subjects of authority in one field play a part in its exercise in others" (Rose 1993, 287). In neoliberal regimes there is also an apparent dispersal of power (Cousins and Hussain 1984) achieved through establishing structures in which professional experts and older people as consumers are co-opted into or coproduce governance through their own accountable and regulated choices. As Burchell (1993) observes, this is directly connected with the political rationality that assigns primacy to marketization and the autonomization of society in which the paradigm of economic action and enterprise culture comes to dominate all forms of conduct, including those areas formerly regarded as noncommercial.

Contrapolitical economy of old age, the very significance of autonomization is that the state appears to relinquish direct control over the actions of public agencies and social policy through a strategy of privatization and insertion of exchange relationships that commodify and monetarize nonmarket welfare goods and services (Burchell 1993). In other words, there is a strategic aim to diffuse the public sector's monolithic power to encourage diversity and fragmentation of provision from public, private, voluntary, and informal modes that is an embodiment of neoliberal policy of maximizing choice for individuals (Powell 2002). Such a strategy, as Rose and Miller (1992) observe, constitutes a fundamental transformation in the mechanisms for governing social life, as it has resulted not only in a rhetorical but a material outcome in their pervasiveness of market disciplines and their objectives of effectiveness, efficiency, and economy.

Marketization thus entails the simultaneous encouragement of consumerism and dependency, the expansion of budgeting and managerial discourse, and structures of accountability in which professional expertise is problematized in new ways. Such technologies of government displace earlier forms with new rationalities of contracts and competition whereby professionals participate in governmentality yet at the same time are themselves subject to intensified forms of regulation and control (Rose 1993).

As Du Gay (1996) has observed, enterprise is a dominant discourse of Western governments, and it has permeated innumerable policies spanning from social welfare to health from the 1980s to the present. Moreover, it has combined two interlinked developments: a stress on the necessity for enterprising subjects or what Burchell terms "responsibilization" (1993, 276) and the resolution of central state control with individual and organizational autonomy, each of which has redefined previous patterns of social relationships within welfare agencies and between those agencies and their older customers/clients. However, while acknowledging the introduction of neoliberal policies to stimulate market modes of action, it is important to recognize, as Burchell (1993) points out, that the implementation of community care is varied, highly contingent, and uncertain. In addition: "the forms of action constructed for schools, hospitals, general practitioners, housing estates, prisons and other social forms are new, invented, and clearly not a simple extension or reproduction of already existing economic forms of action" (Burchell 1993, 275).

Powell (2001d) claims that neoliberal social policies have configured individuals into substrata discourses of the population. For example, social policies explicate "the elderly" as a "clientele" or "consumer" type of people, while statistical and survey knowledges elaborate their status as a demographic entity as an "aging population" discourse. Thus, the formation of subjects as a population makes possible the government of "subjectification" and the cluster of "power/knowledge" that "swarm" around it (Powell 2001d; Biggs and Powell 2001).

While some commentators claim that Foucault rejected monolithic images of the state (Smart 1985), characterized neoliberal government technologies as pluralizing, and conceptualized discipline and power as forms of domination in which subjects are active, governmentality as an analytical construct remains a highly abstract metaphor for a complex and heterogeneous series of interrelated social practices and institutional structures. Hence, the introduction, awareness, and scrutiny of *risk* are core features of a shift in welfare policy from communitarian values to neoliberal individualization and choice. The new emphasis reflects social and cultural changes that give top priority to the construction of self-identity and lifestyle, while negating the collectivist vision of a universalistic welfare state (Gilleard and Higgs 2000).

The controversial point is that governmentality is more complex than state power. Flynn (2002) shows by the example of the Clinical Governance of the National Health Service in Great Britain that it would be too simple to interpret governmentality as a "governing without government." There are no self-organized interorganizational networks with a significant autonomy given by the state or a mixture of different measures that smoothly fit together in a general governmental strategy. Instead, his research on the "clinical governance illustrates the contradictoriness and paradoxes of the management of risk and regulation of professional expertise." On the one hand, the governmentality perspective "allows us to identify the interrelationship of discourses and practices surrounding medical power and state control in the health service—and to see them as being contested and negotiated," but Flynn (2002, 66) emphasizes the need of "intermediate concepts which capture the complexity of organizational change and the process of negotiation." Governmentality may be a totalizing discourse but in practice it is complex and differentiated, dynamic and fluid. It needs to be thought of as permanently incomplete and dependent on an enormously diffuse system of action which itself is the aggregate or structural effect of innumerable interpersonal and organizational transactions. Mark Granovetter (1985) has criticized oversocialized political economistic theories and stressed the importance of socially embedded networks as a way of theorizing relations between macrostructures and microlevels of action. Thus:

> Actors do not behave or decide as atoms outside a social context, nor do they adhere slavishly to a script written for them by the intersection of social categories that they happen to occupy. Their attempts at purposive action are instead embedded in concrete, ongoing systems of social relations. (Granovetter 1985, 487)

In Granovetter's social theory, economic institutions or aging enterprises (cf. Estes 1979) do not emerge automatically; instead, they are socially constructed "by individuals whose action is both facilitated and constrained by the structure and resources available" (1992, 7). Hence, the nature of governmentality in welfare provision are practical accomplishments (people managing their own affairs through self-government) but in their very social construction are contingent upon many forms of contradictory power relations, social actions, and negotiated constraints relating to resources.

This chapter has sketched out the implications for the balance of power/knowledge between professional welfare workers and older people and identified the utopian and dystopian implications of such a divided discourse in Western society. The chapter also links technologies of self with policy spaces with changes in consumer lifestyle that relate to practices of discourse within governmentality. Examples include "technologies of self" evidenced in a growing interest in the maintenance of existing good health, the adoption of retirement community lifestyles (Longino 1994) and the use of "bio" and other forms of technology to modify and in some cases enhance bodily and communicative performance (Shilling 1993). In each case, a technology of the self has been employed in order to reshape the aging self in later life, to overcome or destabilize existing welfare discourses and identity.

THE IMPLICATIONS OF FOUCAULDIAN ANALYSES OF AGING

> It may be that the problem about the self does not have to do with discovering what it is, but maybe has to do with discovering that the self is nothing more than a correlate of technology built into our history.
>
> —Foucault 1988, 222

We spoke earlier of how objectifying technologies of control are, for example, those invented in conformity with the facets of discourses provided by criminality, sexuality, medicine, and psychiatry. These are deployed within concrete institutional settings whose architecture testifies to the "truth" of the objects they contain. Thus the possibilities of self-experience on the part of the subject are, in themselves, affected by the presence of someone who has the authority to decide that they are "truly" ill, such as a "doctor" of medicine (Powell and Biggs 2000). However, "subjectifying" technologies of self-control are those through which individuals: "effect by their own means or with the help of others a certain number of operations on their own bodies and souls, thoughts, conduct and way of being, so as to transform themselves in order to attain a certain state of happiness, purity, wisdom, perfection or immortality" (Foucault 1988, 18).

The important issues that Foucault raises via a questioning of the centrality of the subject are associated to "truthful" formulations of the task or the problem that certain domains of experience and activity pose for older people themselves. Although Foucault maintained the distinction between the discourses and technologies of power/domination and the technologies of self and governmentality, these should not be regarded as acting in opposition to or in isolation from one another. Indeed, Foucault frequently spoke of the importance of considering the contingency of both in their interaction and interdependence, by identifying specific examples: "the point where the technologies of domination of individuals over one another have recourse to processes by which the individual acts upon himself and, conversely, the points where the technologies of the self are integrated into structures of coercion" (Foucault 1988,

203). The distinction should therefore be considered as a heuristic device and not the portrayal of two conflicting sets of interests. Overall, we should see Foucault's entire works as providing ways of understanding social relations that require on our part active interpretation, not passive regurgitation.

Further, what about those questions concerned with whose culture, whose identity, and how is this produced? These are the questions that preoccupied Foucault. His refusal to see power as a property of a particular class immediately leaves a question over his politics in terms of the idea of struggle. As he said: "I label political everything that has to do with class struggle, and social everything that derives from and is a consequence of the class struggle, expressed in human relationships and in institutions" (1988, 104).

This leaves us with a question: against whom do we struggle if not those who hold and exercise power without legitimacy? Who creates cultures and how might alternative forms find public expression, and does this change anything? These questions immediately bring forth issues concerning the relationship between Foucault and political economy of old age that was identified in chapter 3. For example, for Foucault, subjectivity is not a fabricated part of a deeper reality but is itself an aspect of the reality systematically formulated by discourse and power relations. Foucault sidesteps the binary relationship set up by political economy theory (cf. Estes 1979; Estes, Biggs, and Phillipson 2003) between true and false realities, ways of knowing, and political consciousness (Foucault 1980). Nevertheless, Walker (1981) asks the question, "Is not the class structure a key determinant of the position of older individuals in capitalist society?" The implication is that Western society makes "resistance" difficult for older people as a result of a loss of productive roles that put a premium on production (Phillipson 1982). In addition, Foucault's notion of governmentality is problematic itself.

Further, Habermas (1992) claims that Foucault's neo-Nietzscheanist critique of the modernist project fails because he loses a sense of direction. In regard to Foucault (1977), Habermas (1992) accuses him of "crypto-normativity" and "irrationality": the former applies because Foucault cannot explain the standards Habermas thinks must be presupposed in any condemnation of the present; the latter, because of Nietzsche's affirmation of power over against reason.

At the same time, Foucault sees subjectivity not as a fabricated part of a deeper reality waiting to be uncovered through use of reason or communicative rationality (cf. Habermas 1981), but an aspect of the reality systematically formulated by resistances and discourses.

Foucault examined medicine, sexuality, welfare, and selfhood and the law, as well as marginalized social groups, local politics, and the micro-levels of culture. In these studies he found social, discursive, and historical substrata in which relations of domination were apparent that were not simply reducible to modes of economic exploitation. The idea of "governing" then captures the ways in which the "possible fields of action of others" (Foucault 1982, 221) are structured. Yet in inheriting this approach authors have produced panoptic visions in which resistance is subsumed within impersonal forces. This results from overlooking two main aspects in Foucault's work: first, his own question, what are the "limits of appropriation" of discourse"? (Without this in place, all does appear quiet on the battleground); second, and relatedly, the agonism that exists between power and freedom (May 1996). This suggests that where there is power, there is also resistance; power thus presupposes a free subject. If there is no choice in actions, there is no power. A slave, therefore, is not in a power relationship, but one of physical constraint (Foucault 1982).

Foucault notes three types of struggle relevant to understanding aging: those against domination, those against exploitation, and those against subjection and submission. The latter, while rising in importance in the contemporary era, do not do so to the exclusion of domination and exploitation as many of his followers have appeared to suggest. To understand why particular actors enjoy more power than others, as opposed to seeing power as a "machine in which everyone is caught" (Foucault 1980, 156), an account of resistance is needed. Because Foucault views freedom as part of the exercise of power, he does not provide for such an account.

What makes Foucault's overall theoretical work inspiring is how he animates and locates problems of knowledge as "pieces" of the larger contest between modernity and its subjects. By looking at the social construction of the individual subject, Foucault has illuminated how "bodies" and "populations" are sites where "human beings are made subjects" by "power/knowledge" practices (Smart 1993, 44). To look for a possible form of trangression in order to change social relation, we must examine within contemporary arrangements the possibility for it to be "otherwise." We thus find, in Foucault's later work, an insistence upon the reversibility of dominant discourses through "resistance." Subjects of power are also "agents" who can strategically mobilize disjunctures in discourses and, in so doing, open up possibilities in a world that seeks order through discipline and surveillance. Now we begin to see how a situation of one-sided domination can give way to a two-way dialogue without assuming an "essence" to the other that relieves us of the need to understand their worldview. In a time where dominance through military power and money is such a routinized feature of post-9/11 global politics, what greater urgency is there?

CONCLUSION

In his essay on Kant's *Was ist Aufklärung?* (What Is Enlightenment?) Foucault writes of Kant's work as being a "historical ontology of ourselves" through a critique of what we do, say, and think. He is clear throughout the essay concerning what this form of critique is not: neither a theory, doctrine, nor body of knowledge that accumulates over time. Instead, it is an attitude, "an ethos, a philosophical life in which the critique of what we are is at one and the same time the historical analysis of the limits that are imposed on us and an experiment with the possibility of going beyond them" (Foucault 1982, 50). What is the motivation for this work? "How can the growth of capabilities be disconnected from the intensification of power relations?" (1982, 48).

There is no "gesture of rejection" in this ethos. It moves beyond the "outside-inside alternative" in the name of a critique that "consists of analyzing and reflecting upon limits"—the purpose being "to transform the critique conducted in the form of necessary limitation into a practical critique that takes the form of a possible transgression" (Foucault 1982, 45). Overall, it is genealogical in form: "it will not deduce from the form of what we are what it is impossible for us to do and to know; but it will separate out, from the contingency that has made us what we are, the possibility of no longer being, doing, or thinking what we are, do, or think" (1980, 46).

The ideal lies in the possibility of setting oneself free. To examine the internal modes of the ordering of truth, but not in the name of a truth that lies beyond it, is seen to open up possibilities for its transgression.

Despite criticisms that his work lacked a normative dimension (Fraser 1987), the orientation for Foucault's approach is clear. The issue translates into one of how one-sided states of domination can be avoided in order to promote a two-sided relation of dialogue. Foucault's interventions were practically motivated—the journey for these investigations being from how we are constituted as objects of knowledge, to how we are constituted as subjects of power/knowledge. What we can take from Foucault is the insight that critical approaches to gerontological analysis cannot practice on the presupposition that there is an essence to humanity. The idea of coming to know ourselves differently and viewing the possibilities for transformation is about interpreting ourselves differently. Foucault's legacy to understanding aging can be qualified along three lines.

Firstly, gerontology as a "human science" is an *archaeological* domain where discourse, knowledge, and subjectivity engender each other. The "apparatuses" used to disperse gerontological knowledge—discourses, theories, and policies, for example—can be seen as disciplinary techniques that constitute knowledge of subjects/objects.

Secondly, by downplaying the individual subject, Foucault's *genealogies* show how "bodies" and "populations" are sites where "human beings are made subjects" by "power/knowledge" practices (Foucault 1977, 44). The "aging body" and "elderly populations," as the central foci of scientific knowledge, cultural images, political rationalities, and institutional practices, have organized the positioning of later life.

Thirdly, there is an ontological reflexivity within Foucault's later work whereby he insists on the reversibility of discourses by subjects through *technologies of self* and "resistance." Older people are subjects of power who are also "agents" who could strategically mobilize disjunctures of structural discourses through "technologies of self" (Foucault 1978; Biggs and Powell 2001).

Indeed, by using such distinctive methodologies of archaeology and genealogy, and technologies of self, Foucault reveals relations of power and power relationships between professionals, institutions, and subjects of study while demonstrating their relevance to uncovering discourses relating to construction of knowledge about the nature of individuality and control of such knowledge bases.

While Foucault has provided us with conceptual insights that enrich understanding of discourses of aging and professional power, the notion of risk is an undeveloped theme in his work. The notion of risk is fundamental to the way experts experience and organize the social world. Risk is crucial to the understanding and control of the future (Beck 1992). The central yet uncertain nature of risk and risk assessment is pivotal to understanding the changing nature and role of power/knowledge and professional experts in contemporary society (Beck 1992). Risks come into being where traditions and assumed values such as social work as a form of expertise have deteriorated (Powell and Biggs 2000). As Beck states: "The concept of risk is like a probe which permits us over and over again to investigate the entire construction plan, as well as every individual speck of cement in the structure of civilization" (1992, 176).

The emergence of a risk society arises because of the undermining and loss of faith concerning power/knowledge and hierarchies of truth and expert systems. It is not by chance, then, that the increased focus on risk in social work coincided with the decline in trust in health and welfare professionals' expertise, decision-making, and scientific-medical insights on aging and the growing reliance on the managerial gaze with older people in post-welfare societies. The next chapter looks at the implications of the "risk society" for understanding aging in contemporary society.

6

Aging in the "Risk Society"

INTRODUCTION

This chapter explores the relationship of aging to the concept of "risk" that is both an epistemological tool and major facet of "late modernity" (Delanty 1999; Giddens 1991). During the 1970s, the use of the notion of risk was mainly confined to "natural sciences," where the concept was used to analyze and improve the "security" of technological systems (Giddens 1990). According to Lupton (1999) it was not until the 1980s and 1990s that social science–based disciplines discovered the importance of risk in relation to changes affecting modern society. In particular, the disciplinary development of sociology, for example, has discovered risk as one of the important aspects of neoliberalism and modernity (Beck 1992; Giddens 1990; Luhmann 1993; Delanty 1999). The best-known approach in recent sociology of risk is the perspective of "risk society" (Beck 1992). This approach had a very large initial impact, but conceptual and empirical critiques have developed subsequently. Sociocultural research suggests the idea of a subject that is itself strongly influenced by its cultural context, and builds up its own risk-knowledge referring to different, competing, and sometimes contradictory knowledge systems which are available in different life situations and stages. For this reason, expert knowledge is only one point of reference among others (Delanty 1999). People build up such "private" knowledge on the base of their experiences during their life-course and in interaction with their contexts—others, the media, science, and expert knowledge (Wilkinson 2001).

Indeed, in contemporary Western society, risk is a broad concept that extends over a broad range of social practices that impinge on the experiences of older people. Current debates about older people and their relationship to sexuality, crime, national security, food safety, employment, and welfare are all underscored by risk (Phillipson 1998). Moreover, there is an increasing recognition that potential risks of the present and future—global warming, genetic cloning, genetically modified foods, and bioterrorism—shatter the rigid boundaries of nations and demand global cooperation and control.

Awareness of the transboundary nature of risk has led the United Nations to form its own Commission on Human Security. A recent report by the UN Commission suggests ways in which the security of older people, for example, might be advanced—from humanitarian and military strategies through to economic, health, and educational strategies. While "freedom from want" continues to be the most pressing global imperative, in recent years "freedom from fear" has risen up the global political agenda (Commission on Human Security 2003, 4, cited in Powell and Wahidin 2004). Coupled with this, the U.S. Central Intelligence Agency's 2004 *World Fact Book* suggests that an "aging population" is a risk to the financial safety of Western nation-states (Powell and Wahidin 2004).

In science, risk has traditionally been approached as an objective material entity, to be mastered by processes of calculation, assessment, and probability. In the twenty-first century, "advances" in science and medicine led to the eradication of many infectious diseases, raised life expectancy in old age, and improved quality of life. Accordingly, it is no surprise that the literature on risk was housed within the confines of specialist expert disciplines, such as biomedical gerontology (Timiras 1997).

The nature of scientific knowledge about risk and its impact on aging has articulated the perspective that, as a person goes through the aging process, there are heightened risks to the human body—in the mind and in the internal organs (Hughes 1995). It has gradually become clear that the very institutions entrusted with regulating risks have themselves transmuted into risk producers. In recent times, multinational corporate business, science, medicine, and government have all been accused of generating various dangers to public health that threaten the safety of older people. The rising cultural profile of risk has brought to the fore deep-rooted ethical concerns about the relationship between individuals, institutions, and society (Lupton 1999, 112). The debate currently taking place about the use of reproductive technologies for human cloning to prolong life in old age stands as a case in point. Such situations indicate that—in addition to being a scientific and economic issue—risk is now also interpreted as both a social and political issue.

It has become commonplace for academics and practitioners to explore, develop, and apply an assortment of social science perspectives on risk. In a post-9/11 world, questions around risk and risk management have become ever more pertinent, leading to reflections on a number of different levels about "ontological security." Moreover, how do older people manage their sense of well-being in a world in which less and less can be taken for granted? To what extent does the specter of global risks interplay with more mundane insecurities that reach to the capillary texture of the day-to-day life of older people?

In a climate of indeterminacy, there is an urgent need to draw out the ways in which wider social theory can elucidate the dynamic relationship between risk and aging in contemporary society. In response to public concerns about unbounded technoscientific development and the apparent inefficacy of expert systems, interest in risk has gathered momentum within social science disciplines in recent years (cf. Giddens 1991). However, while the language of risk has become prolific, the concept itself remains cloaked in ambiguity and its relationship to aging scantily researched; making risk and aging an important and significant issue for social theory and social gerontology.

A theoretically informed understanding of risk illustrates the interconnectedness of an "aging population," social policy and social life. From this perspective, risk is more than an estimation of costs and benefits; it is a theoretical instrument for weighing dissimilar sets of values and political orientations that affect the positioning of individuals and populations. As Nikolas Luhmann (1993, ix) points out:

> How do we comprehend our society if we turn the concept of risk into a universal problem neither avoidable or evadable? What is now necessary? And accordingly: What is chance? How does society in the normal performance of its operations cope with a future about which nothing certain can be discerned, but only what is more or less probable or improbable?

The deployment of risk to gerontological contexts has facilitated disruptions of both the metanarratives inscribed within gerontology, as both discipline and policy, and the ontological status of its subjects, that is, older people. The rationale for this argument is not about a normative foundation for articulating agency afforded to older people. Part of an understanding of individual freedom is how human action is plugged into and (de)regulated by a *social context* (Mills 1959). Such an approach seeks to capture the dimensions of subjectivity within the sociopolitical constraints that shape individual lives. This allows reconstructions of logics of action or structuration behind current neoliberal self-representations of aging identity. It could be supposed that such constructions enable us to reconstruct the complexity of aging in social contexts and the influence of, for example, social welfare on these experiences as a ground for risk perception.

Hence, we need to understand the major *social forces* that impinge on aging itself. Such social forces that create risk associated with aging imply a breakdown in *trust* as a key modernist principle in contemporary society.

FROM TRUST TO RISK

There are increasing attempts to conceptualize the notion of "trust" in social theory as a pivotal dimension of modernity (Giddens 1991). Trust is incompatible, on the one hand, with complete ignorance of the possibility and probability of future events, and, on the other hand, with emphatic belief, when the anticipation of disappointment is excluded. Someone who trusts has an expectation directed to an event. The expectations are based on the ground of incomplete knowledge about the probability and incomplete control about the occurrence of the event. Trust is of relevance for action and has consequences for the trusting agent if trust is confirmed or disappointed. Thus, trust is connected with risk (Giddens 1991).

Up to now there have been few attempts to work out a systematic scheme of different forms of trust between older people and individuals, institutions, or policies that have bearing on their identity performance. Social trust tends to be high among older people who believe that their public safety is high (Wahidin and Powell 2001). As public trust erodes regarding institutions like the government and the media (Phillipson 1998), trust attracts more and more attention in social sciences.

Mölling (2001) distinguishes between trust in contracts between people and state, such as pension provision; trust in friendships across intergenerational lines; trust in love and relationships; and trust in foreign issues associated with national identity. However, sociological theories that suppose a general change in modernity (cf. Beck 1992) assume that, with the erosion of traditional institutions and scientific knowledge, trust becomes an issue more often produced actively by individuals than institutionally guaranteed.

Independent from the insight that social action in general is dependent more or less on trust, empirical results in the context of risk perception and risk taking indicate:

- Trust is much easier to destroy than to build.
- Once trust is undermined, it is more difficult to restore it.
- Familiarity with a place, a situation, or a person produces trust.
- People will develop trust in other people or situations if those people or situations have positively valued characteristics.

Trust seems to be something that is produced individually by experience and over time and cannot be immediately and with purpose be produced by organizations or governments without dialogical interaction with older people on issues affecting their lifestyles and life-chances such as care, pensions, employment, and political representation (Walker and Naeghele 1999). However, as Giddens (1991) stresses, risk is a feature of a society shifting its emphasis away from trust in traditional ties and social values. How risks are perceived and formulated as a breakdown in trust reflects the essentially discursive practices of politics and power in modern society. The ability to control and manage perceptions about moral intentions of a pervasive governmental rationality may be part of an understanding of risk.

For this reason, risk is an evocative and compelling focus of theoretical analysis, requiring for understanding a historical backdrop for the emergence of a risk society in the West that influences the identities of older people.

THE HISTORICAL RISE AND CONSOLIDATION OF "RISK"

Over history, the word *risk* has changed its meaning and has become far more common applied to the global and the local (Beck 1992). Most commentators link the emergence of the word and concept of risk with early maritime ventures in the premodern period. Ewald (1993) argues that the notion of risk first appeared in the Middle Ages, related to maritime insurance, and alluded to the perils that could compromise a voyage: "At that time, risk designated the possibility of an objective danger, an act of God, a force, a tempest or other peril of the sea that could not be imputed to wrongful conduct" (Ewald 1993, 226).

Luhmann (1993, 9) claims that the German word for risk appeared in the mid-sixteenth century and the English, in the second half of the seventeenth. He notes that the Latin term *riscum* had been in use long before in Germany and elsewhere.

Importantly, this premodern concept of risk excluded the idea of human fault and responsibility. Risk was perceived to be a natural event, such as a storm, flood, or epidemic, rather than a human-made one. By the eighteenth century, the concept of risk had begun to be rationalized under the new scientific paradigm, drawing upon new ideas of mathematical probability. The development of statistical calculations of risk and the expansion of the insurance industry in the early modern era meant that: "Consequences that at first affect only the individual became 'risks,' systematically caused, statistically describable and in that sense 'predictable' types of events, which can therefore also be subjected to supraindividual and political rules of recognition, compensation and avoidance" (Beck 1992, 99).

By the late nineteenth century, the notion of risk was extended. It was no longer located exclusively in nature but was "also in human beings, in their conduct, in their liberty, in the relations between them, in the fact of their association, in society" (Ewald 1993, 226). The development of this concept assumes human responsibility and that "something can be done" to prevent misfortune. Feelings of insecurity are common, just as they were in premodern times, but we now harbor somewhat different fears, and different objects are causes for our anxiety.

As in premodern times, we are aware of certain types of risks and possible outcomes, but our responses are more governed by a scientific rationale. The symbolic basis of our uncertainties is fundamentally created by disorder or insecurities, such as the loss of control over our bodies, our relationship with others and self, and the extent to which we can exert autonomy in our everyday lives. This body of governance or strategies can take many forms, from dieting, to fitness regimes to minimizing potential risk to self by taking out life insurance, installing a burglar alarm, etc. These are just some of the ways by which the heightened awareness of everyday risk is negotiated, contained, and managed. Therefore, rational thinking, systems of prevention, and ways of identifying threats before they take effect are means of managing danger and threats in a risk society. These strategies are the products of late modern ways of thinking about, and reacting to, risk.

> Every technology produces, provokes, programmes a specific accident . . . . The invention of the boat was the invention of shipwrecks. The invention of the steam engine and the locomotive was the invention of derailments. The invention of the highway was the invention of three hundred cars colliding in five minutes. The invention of the airplane was the invention of the plane crash. I believe that from now on, if we wish to continue with technology (and I don't think there will be a Neolithic regression), we must think about both the substance and the accident. (Virilio 1983, 32)

The modernist concept of risk represented a new way of viewing the world and its chaotic manifestations, its contingencies and uncertainties. It assumed that unanticipated outcomes may be the consequence of human action rather than "expressing the hidden meanings of nature or ineffable intentions of the Deity," largely replacing earlier concepts of fate or *fortuna* (Giddens 1990, 30).

As Reddy argues: "Moderns had eliminated genuine indeterminacy, or 'uncertainty,' by inventing 'risk.' They had learnt to transform a radically indeterminate cosmos into a manageable one, through the myth of calculability" (Reddy 1996, 237). Castel goes even further, arguing that the obsession with the prevention of risk in modernity is built upon:

> a grandiose technocratic rationalizing dream of absolute control of the accidental, understood as the irruption of the unpredictable . . . a vast hygienist utopia plays on the alternate registers of fear and security, inducing a delirium of rationality, an absolute reign of calculative reason and a no less absolute prerogative of its agents, planners and technocrats, administrators of happiness for a life to which nothing happens. (Castel 1991, 289)

In modernity, risk, in its purely technical meaning, came to rely upon conditions in which the probability estimates of an event are able to be known or knowable. The use of risk in common discourse litters texts, images, and day-to-day conversation. In contemporary Western societies, the noun *risk* and the adjective *risky* have become very commonly used in both popular and expert discourses. Risk and uncertainty tend to be treated as conceptually the same thing. The term tends to be used to refer almost exclusively to a threat, hazard, danger, or harm: we "risk our life savings" by investing on the stock exchange, or we "put our health at risk." The term is also used to refer to a somewhat negative rather than disastrous outcome, as in the warning, "if you go out without your coat, you'll risk catching a cold." In this sense, risk means somewhat less than a possible danger or a threat and more an unfortunate or annoying event. Risk is therefore a very loose term and, as the above shows, is used in a variety of ways. Issues of calculable probability and economic systems of accountability are not necessarily important to the colloquial use of risk. Risk knowledges are historical and local, in the literature known as *glocal*. What might be perceived to be "risky" in one era at a certain locale may no longer be so viewed later, or in a different place (Phillipson and Powell 2004). As a result, risk knowledges are constantly contested, subject to disputes and debates over their nature, their control, and who is to blame for their creation.

Over time the constellations of risks have changed. The risks of early industrialization were evident—they could be smelt, touched, tasted, or observed with the naked eye. These hazards "assaulted the nose or the eyes and were thus perceptible to the senses" (Beck 1992, 21). Earlier risks were part of a system of stratification and poverty that was highly visible; in contrast, today's hazards are invisibly everywhere in the everyday. Many of the major risks today largely escape perception "for they are localized in the sphere of physical and chemical formulas (e.g., toxins in foodstuffs, toxins in the environment, [certain pollutants] or nuclear threat)" (Beck 1992, 21). These risks exist in scientific knowledge rather than in everyday experience. Expert knowledges tend to contradict each other, resulting in debates over standpoints, calculation, assessment procedures, and results. This has the effect of paralyzing action and bringing insurance systems that promised to cover eventualities into chaos. In Great Britain, for example, the welfare state, an insurance system that promised to care for people from cradle to the grave, is unable to sustain that promise for future generations. The welfare system as a system of social insurance is beginning to lose its legitimacy with the rise of private health insurance.

Scientists have lost their authority in relation to risk assessments, most evidently seen in the collapse of endowment and certain pension funds.

Scientific calculations are challenged more and more by political groups and activist (Beck 1994, 125–26). The nature of such hazards, therefore, returns the concept of risk to the premodern notion of "incalculable insecurities." In common with such hazards, insecurities "undercut the social logic of risk calculation and provision" (Beck 1994, 77). For Beck, then, risk may be defined as a "systematic way of dealing with hazards and insecurities induced and introduced by modernisation itself" (Beck 1992, 21). Dangers and hazards in modern society are the cause and effect of humanly generated productions and in essence can be avoided, monitored, or altered. Therefore the above debates demonstrate that the essence of risk is not that it *is* happening, but that it *might* be happening.

These debates include "reflexive modernisation" (cf. Giddens 1991), or the move toward criticism of the outcomes of neoliberalism, and individualization, or the breaking down of traditional norms and values. Older people living in neoliberal societies have therefore moved toward a greater awareness of risk and are forced to deal with risks on an everyday basis: "Everyone is caught up in defensive battles of various types anticipating the hostile substances in one's manner of living and eating" (Beck 1992, 45). The media, for their part, have taken up warnings of experts about risk and communicate them to their mass publics. They have also reported disputes among these experts that concern risks: how serious they are; who should be blamed for them; what the most appropriate course of action might be. In risk society, therefore, the politics and sub-politics of risk definition become extremely important. They highlight the contested nature of who is defining what is a risk and how. Various specialized fields have developed around "risk." Our understanding of risk derives from pervasive references to risk behavior, risk awareness, risk analysis, risk assessment, risk communication, and risk management—among other notions—at any given time. Such terms allude to major fields of research and practice, developed in an attempt to measure, evaluate, and regulate risk in areas as far-ranging as medicine, law, education, social policy, and health, but they also signify the techniques by which, as social actors, we come to make sense of the everyday. In the last few years, there has been a series of "panics" about welfare resources that has revolved around particular items in the United Kingdom, such as the effects of an "aging population" on public resources and taxation. Thus, perceptions of risk are intimately tied to understandings of what constitutes a danger and for whom. This im/materiality or the invisibility gives risk an air of un-reality until the moment at which they materialize as symptoms or as ir-reversible side effects.

The growing disparities between rich countries and poorer ones lead to growing inequalities in risk distribution, where class positions and risk positions overlap. As we see these disparities develop in the new global order, some risks, such as those caused by hazardous industries, are transferred away from the developed countries to the Third World. Thus, while Beck sees risk society as a catastrophic society, what we are seeing is the transference of certain risks through aversion and manage-ment, which in turn include a *reorganization of power and authority* (Beck 1992, 4)

THE "RISK SOCIETY" THESIS

Beck (1992) in his work *Risk Society* acknowledges that some social groups are more affected than others by the distribution and growth of risks, and these differences may be structured through inequalities of class and social position. The disadvantaged have fewer opportunities to avoid risk because of their comparative lack of resources. By contrast, the wealthy to a degree (income, power, or education) can purchase safety and freedom from risk (Beck 1992, 33). However, it is the gesta-tion and the constellations of the risks that are unknown, and thus risk also affects those who have produced or profited from them, breaking down the previous social and geographic boundaries evident in modern societies.

Beck argues that the "former colonies" of the Western nations are soon becoming the waste dumps of the world for toxic and nuclear wastes produced by more privileged countries. Risks have become more and more difficult to calculate and control. Hence it can be argued that risks often affect both the wealthy and poor alike: "poverty is hierarchic and smog is democratic" (1992, 36). At the same time, because of the de-gree of interdependence of the highly specialized agents of moderniza-tion in business, agriculture, the law and politics, there is no single agent responsible for any risk: "[T]here is a general complicity, and the com-plicity is matched by a general lack of responsibility. Everyone is cause *and* effect" (33) and so "perpetrator and victim become identical" (38) in a consuming society. It is this im/materiality and in/visibility of the threats that saturate the "risk society," making it harder to identify the offender in global risk. Lupton (1999) argues that this fundamentally poses the second challenge for analyses of these socially constituted industrial phenomena: interpretation becomes inherently a matter of perspective and hence political. Politicians constantly invoke science in their attempts to persuade the public that their policies and products are safe. The inescapability of interpretation makes risks infinitely malleable and, as Beck (1992, 23) insists, "open to social definition and construction." This in turn put those in a position to define (and/or legitimate) risks—the mass media, scientists, politicians, and the legal profession—in key social positions.

"Risk society," argues Beck, *"is not an option* which could be chosen or rejected in the course of political debate" (1996, 28, *Authors italics*). Instead, this is an inescapable product and structural condition of advance industrialization in which the produced hazards of that system, in Beck's words (1992, 31), "undermine and/or cancel the established safety systems of the provident state's existing risk calculation." Beck (1992) in his work further emphasizes this point by examining contemporary hazards associated with nuclear power, chemical pollution, and genetic engineering and biotechnology that cannot be limited or contained to particular spaces, and that which cannot be grasped through the rules of causality, and cannot be safeguarded, compensated for, or insured against. They are therefore "glocal": both local and global. Risk society is thus "world risk society," and risks affect a global citizenship. The questioning of the outcomes of modernity in terms of the production of risks is an outcome of reflexive modernization. Our awareness of risk, therefore, is heightened at the level of the everyday.

Both Beck (1992) and Giddens (1991) have a commonality of exploring and assessing risk linked to personal conduct and ontological security. Both claim that modernization helps the self become an agent via processes of individualization which they both see as indicative of neoliberalism; they advocate that the self become less constrained by structures and become a project to be reflexively worked on.

Further studies refer to general discourses and their influence of problem definitions and the constitution of groups "at risk" as older people (Estes, Biggs, and Phillipson 2003). Such studies show how generalized social categories in institutional and media discourses produce homogenous groups in relation to risk. On the one hand, these categories do not do justice to the diverse persons behind the categories, and a new reality is entailed that changes the whole notion of a social group. For example, risk anxiety engendered by the desire to keep older people safe may restrict their autonomy and their opportunities to develop necessary skills to cope with the world.

Notwithstanding this, there is a criticism that "risk" is narrowed to the responses of technical and environmental risks as unforeseen consequences of industrialization. This concept of a *danger-consequence society* (Massumi 1993) fails to grasp the more general societal development regarding the concept of risk as a specific historical strategy to manage uncertainties. This strategy is strongly linked to the idea of insurance and the statistical methods to calculate uncertainties developed in modernity (Hacking 1990). Many risk theorists share this view (Giddens 1991) but support a more general notion on risk and risk responses in current societies concerning the ways in which uncertainties of aging populations are managed in general. The narrowed view on technical and statistical risk management seems to be insufficient for the given complexity concerning, for example, governmental risk strategies and rationalities (Rose 1996) and emotional spaces. Further critique aims at the assumption that new risks produce a general anxiety that would support a higher public awareness of risk and involve increasing the political commitment of the public. It has been argued that this does not apply to all risks, and neither do all people respond in the same way (Lupton 1999).

The existing literature on risk ignores the role of *emotion* in theorizing. Often it is assumed without further empirical examination that there is a direct link between social structure and emotion or risk consciousness and societal anxiety of "emotions." One clear example of risk associated with emotions and aging is crime and victimization. As with other characteristics that make older people vulnerable to victimization, it is difficult to disentangle the age factor from other variables that mean that older people figure prominently among those for whom victimization has a high risk. In terms of actual rates of victimization, elder abuse is certainly underreported (Biggs 1993). Many older people may feel vulnerable related to crime and abuse (Wahidin and Powell 2001). Older victims tend to report that crime has a high and long-lasting impact upon them compared to younger victims.

Fattah and Sacco (1989) conclude in their study of crime against older people in North America that:

While it may be fashionable to view fear of crime as an irrational response on the part of elderly to a world that does not truly threaten them, such a conceptualisation is probably not appropriate. Rather than irrationality, elderly fear of crime may represent the exercise of caution by a group in society that frequently lacks the control necessary to manage the risk of criminal harm or to marshal the resources necessary to offset its consequences. (1989, 226)

Hence, the multilayered results of the link between risk, crime, and emotion show that additional theoretical work in social gerontology is necessary. Wahidin and Powell (2001) refer to the idea of a fundamental change in modernity—that there is also a reinterpretation of the uncontrollable and unforeseeable in something observable such as crime.

AGING IN RISK SOCIETY:
A CASE STUDY BASED ON SOCIAL WELFARE

Throughout risk literature there has been a growing gap in the application of risk in gerontology. Notwithstanding this, in order to work on itself, the "self" relates to risk: "risks become the motor of *self-politicization* of modernity in industrial society." How the conjunction between risk and individual awareness has become politicized provides a perspective on the viability of neoliberalism and conditions of human action. One element of the "motor" of self-politicization is how successful neoliberalism has been in fashioning *commonsense* discourses around its political rhetoric. Jürgen Habermas (1992) claims that what we are witnessing is a "completely altered relationship between autonomous and self-organized public spheres on the one hand, and sub-systems steered by money and administrative power on the other." *Self-autonomization* coupled with *administrative power* is indicative of "risk": neoliberal features of social policy for older people.

There is then an ambivalence at the heart of neoliberalism: on the one hand, older people are to be "managed" by other administrative powers such as professional experts in modernity (Leonard 1997); on the other hand, older people are left to govern themselves, a process that Rose and Miller (1992) call "action at a distance" from the state. Hence, as consumers, older people are distanced further away from the state; rather than a cause for celebration, the dystopian implications are far-reaching in that they generate further risks that the self must negotiate with the withdrawal of the state.

Indeed, constituting risk as a centrally defining motif of "late modernity" offers a new perspective: it allows the interrogation of how older people are made subjects. This inevitably impinges on risk. Neoliberalism gives the impression that older people have the capacity to generate their own "human agency" as indicative of "consumer culture" (Gilleard and Higgs 2000) irrespective of structural constraints. The problematic of self-governance, or what Nikolas Rose (1993) calls "the government of freedom," needs critical reflection. Such reflection is sensitized to mapping out key features of neoliberal political rationalities that impinge on "self-government" within the "risk society"—notably those arising from the shift from welfarism to neoliberalism.

We can draw from neoliberal features of social policy to highlight how old age was socially and politically positioned as an opportunity for processes of government related to self-governance (Rose 1993, 1996). Theoretical normativity lies at the heart of the "structure vs. agency" debate as applied to social gerontology. Social gerontology as discipline and practice can be sensitized to how older people *ought to* have autonomy and control in their own lives; but this masks critical questions of the *what is*. As Powell (1998) asks, how do we know where we are going until we know where we are coming from? So, we point out features of the "risk society" and how this impacts on any historical, contemporary, and future questioning of aging.

The next section traces a genealogy of aging, risk, and its interrelationship with social welfarism.

GENEALOGY OF RISK AND AGING IDENTITIES

There has been a change in the structure that has underpinned definitions of aging. The key development here concerned the way in which, in industrial societies, growing old was altered by the social and economic institutions connected with the welfare state. These became crucial in shaping the dominant discourse around which aging was framed. A key theme was the reordering of the life-course into life zones associated with education, work, and retirement (Phillipson 1982). A final element concerned the role played by services for older people as a measure of the move to a more civilized society. "Old age" was itself the creation of modernity, reflecting the achievements of industrialism, improved public health, and the growth of social welfare (Biggs 1999). The steady growth in the proportion of older people in the population was, until the beginning of the 1980s, largely contained within the institution of the welfare state.

Indeed, older people have had the most to lose, given the restructuring of relationships associated with the emergence of a postmodern society. As Biggs (1993) argues, modern life raises at least two possibilities: the promise of a multiplicity of identities on the one side, and the danger of psychological disintegration on the other. This development has served to change the definition of what it means to be an older person. In the conditions of advanced modernity, growing old moves from being a collective to an individual experience and responsibility. This new development may be seen as a characteristic of a society in which the "social production of risk" runs alongside that associated with the "social production of wealth" (Beck 1992). Beck (1992, 21) further defines the nature of risk as a *"systematic way of dealing with hazards and insecurities induced and introduced by modernization itself"* [emphasis supplied]. Such modernization is shaped by neoliberalism which in turn positions the role and responsibility of what it means to be a consumer in Western society.

CONCLUSION

The neoliberal *surface* dominance in social policy has been very successful because it has identified existential concepts such as self-responsibility, self-governance, and self-care which are to be used to facilitate human action and self-government (Powell 2001c, 2001d). The regulation of personal conduct is no longer the responsibility of the state.

Here neoliberal discourse attempts to define the social policy domain to interpret valid human needs and limit rights, indicative of risk. Coupled with this, processes and relationships in the management of old age are decided by governmental rationalities that are tied to questions of self-governance, self-actualization, and autonomy. Further, neoliberalism considers that a welfare society must reflect only the interplay of social and political structures forged out of self-responsibility and consumerism (Leonard 1997; Powell 2001e). As we discussed in a previous chapter regarding analysis of Foucault's (1978) notion of "governmentality," older people as *autonomous* consumers derive their "care," individually and collectively, from a range of social policies, institutions, and sites, so that the organization of care involves market forces, families, and state and care institutions. In the United States, responsibility for the *administration* of care-based social policy has been the contemporary case management institution (Powell 2001d).

Case management as an institutional apparatus has been presented as consolidating neoliberalism by adding "choice" and reducing "risks" and "problems" associated with aging. This movement away from "helping relationship" to "care management" is an aspect of governance—the mechanism by which clients, as individuals and collectively, are "disciplined" away from "structured dependency" to the governance of "self" in the "risk society" (Powell 2001). Such reforms were about recasting older people as consumers in a marketplace to be managed by administrative powers (Powell 2001; cf. Habermas 1992).

Indeed, Biggs and Powell (2001, 110) raise critical questions about the relationship between old age, neoliberalism, and new sources of oppression associated with the risk society:

> Those who do not conform to the utopian dream appear to have been shunted into a non-participative discourse, bounded by professional surveillance or the more palatable yet closely related discourse of "monitoring." In both cases, it could be suggested that a discourse on dependency has been supplemented, and in some cases replaced, by a discourse on risk. The risk of giving in to an aging body, the risk of thereby being excluded from one's retirement community, the risk of being too poor to maintain a consumer lifestyle, the risk of being excluded from participation through incapacity that has been externally assessed, the risk of being abused, the risk of control being taken out of one's hands, and the risk of tokenism in partnership.

Risk is then much more than a calculation of costs and benefits, it is a *theoretical* endeavor whereupon what seems to be a simple question such as "Do we live in a risk society?" is one to which we are incapable of providing a straight answer. As consumers, has our duty of care become onerous or riskier as we journey into the stages of later life? Can anyone escape the miasma of a risk? As Phillipson and Powell (2004) critically suggest:

> Older people, it might be argued, are affected by two major changes: in respect of access to support on the one side, and the construction of identity

on the other. On the one side, there is the creation of what Estes and others describe as "No Care Zones" where community supports may disintegrate in the face of inadequate services and benefits. On the other side, there may equally be the emergence of "No Identity Zones," these reflecting the absence of spaces in which to construct a viable identity for older people. (Phillipson and Powell 2004, 55)

The lack of spaces adds to a sense of marginalization that exposes the vulnerable status of older people. But this vulnerability is not just about the material experience of deprivation; it also reaches into the texture of everyday life. For more affluent groups, a temporary solution seems to have been found in the denial of aging and the neoliberal promotion of new consumer lifestyles. The social vacuum that this suggests reinforces the sense of uncertainty about the identity of older people in neoliberal consumer society (Phillipson 1998).

7

Conclusion

Reconstructions of Aging

Throughout this book we have critically questioned taken-for-granted assumptions about aging and old age. The book aimed to provide a critical reflection to ideas and concepts of social theory and relevance to aging studies so as to facilitate understanding of modernist perspectives through to postmodern dimensions of human aging.

The discussion began with an assessment of the *modern constructions of aging*. In chapter 2, we analyzed the master narratives of aging into old age, with a focus on biomedical conceptualizations of mind/body "decline" (Cassel 1991). As was illuminated, in Occidental culture in particular, the aging body is the baseline, subject to relentless forces of negative decline (Powell 2001d). Insofar as there is a history of aging, there is also a history of efforts to control and regulate older people (Powell and Biggs 2000). The master narrative of natural decline of aging bodies hides the location of complex intersections of negative ideas that comprise an aging culture (Biggs and Powell 2000; Longino and Powell 2004). We revealed how a key contribution of social theory as a broad discipline has been to highlight how individual lives and behavior, once thought to be determined solely by biology and psychology (Powell 2001a; Cassel 1991), are, in fact, heavily influenced by social environments in which people live and hence are *socially constructed*.

In chapter 3, we traced how the adverse quality of life experienced by many older people was caused by: the effects of modern capitalism that

impinge on retirement process (Phillipson 1998), particularly gender oppression through materiality and patriarchy (Arber and Ginn 1995). For
functionalist gerontology, however, the social situation of older people
should be one whereby the person either stays "active" or "disengages."
Such theories that highlight modernist narratives have held intellectual respectability in terms of "cause and effect"—for example, "you retire and
then you disengage" (cf. Cumming and Henry 1961)—the master disengagement epistemic narrative.

The second part of the book used a critical approach to denote ways of
thinking to continually challenge the taken-for-grantedness of modernity
and open up the possibility for understanding aging through alternative
yet postmodern *deconstructions of aging*. For Seidman (1994, 317) to ignore a shift toward a postmodernism would be "a grave mistake." In assessing the implications of postmodernism for social theory and aging
studies, it is important to give postmodernism the credit it deserves and
take note of both the epistemological and ontological possibilities it allows for sociological theorizing at localistic levels in everyday life (Seidman 1994). For example, we looked at three areas of postmodern deconstructions of aging: (1) understanding aging body and culture; (2)
power/knowledge relations between older people and professional experts; (3) aging in the risk society.

The contemporary cultural, political, economic, and scientific representations of aging within Western culture are, as a result of these deconstructions, becoming increasingly important in social discourses on aging,
both in the disciplines of social theory and social gerontology and in the
policies and practices of institutions that attempt to define later life
(Phillipson 1998).

In chapter 4, the discussion turned to how the intrasubjective aging
body has been positioned in postmodern popular culture through
biotechnological reconstruction. The postmodern analysis of the aging
body is important in restoring the body to interconnected disciplines
such as social theory and social gerontology. However, the emphasis on
body gender has ebbed and flowed in the sociological imaginary as "female corporeality" and "male embodiment." In a parallel discourse, the
book maintains that emergent constructions of aging are becoming increasingly fluid (Gilleard and Higgs 2000), in the process eroding many
of the modernist "decline" meanings traditionally associated with old
age, but it has also left aging people rootless and prone to increasing uncertainty and "risk."

Alongside this, chapters 5 and 6 highlighted how "social welfare" is a key example of where social discourses on aging have become situated that impinge on the intersubjective dimensions of historical and contemporary everyday life between professional experts and older people based on "power/knowledge," "governmentality," and "technologies of self" (Foucault 1988) and risk (Giddens 1991; Beck 1992). We assessed the discourse of "social welfare" as a key example of a medium used to legitimize and position the identities that older people adopt in contemporary Western societies. It contains recurrently variable technologies that function to reconcile relations between older people and the state. Medico-technical and "case management" neoliberal discourses have been presented as adding choice and reducing boundaries associated with adult aging. However, as discussed in chapter 5, they also represent an amplification of professional control that can be coerced on lifestyles in older age. As Shrag (1980, 252) points out:

> It is a subtle, erosive process. Almost every agency of education, social welfare and mental health talks the seductive language of prevention, diagnosis and treatment; and almost every client is a hostage to an exchange which trades momentary comfort and institutional peace for an indefinite future of maintenance and control.

At the same time, aging appears to be moving from its traditional concern with "public issues" to the question of how aging is individualized in neoliberal Western societies through governmentality and postmodern culture (Katz 2000). This is particularly apparent in a move toward social discourses of consumerism, which appears to indicate a shift of attention from responding to discrete macroproblems (cf. Townsend 1981) to an attempt to problematize what constitutes the "aging body" and wider questions of embodiment, corporeality, and reflexivity (Biggs and Powell 2001; Powell and Longino 2002). This postmodern trend has the potential to intensely reconstruct both formal expectations and personal experiences of aging itself (Calasanti 1996).

The pertinent question to raise is, has this been theorized adequately? The answer is that the relationship between social theory and the study of aging has become closely entwined, leading critical gerontologists such as Estes, Biggs, and Phillipson (2003) to question the "commonsense assumptions" that may be held there.

The change to *constructing, deconstructing,* and *reconstruc*ting an aging identity is partially due to the erosion of values and assumptions of
modernity and to the move toward the "risk society" (Beck 1992). Here,
aging identities have traditionally depended upon policy discourses
within and between professions and institutions of the state in Western
culture (Donzelot 1979, 1988).

We could argue that the experience of the welfare state has been ambivalent, insofar as it often provides people with what they need but in
ways that erode a positive sense of self. However, a perceived oxidiza-
tion of these structures has led to an interiorization of the position
upon which a feasible aging identity can be built. This is reflected in a
postmodern interest in the use of "masking" of aging performativity
(Featherstone and Hepworth 1993). This has been accompanied by a
deconstruction of biomedical discourses of "decline" and "withdrawal"
and the promotion of models of "consumer aging" (Estes, Biggs, and
Phillipson 2003). Indeed, part of the seductive array of discourses in consumer culture centers on self-subjectification lifestyles. These discourses,
which impinge on aging, have thereby taken on a "normative" dimension, which mediates a daily understanding of what it is to age through
the life-course.

At the same time, we are alerted to the narrow-minded nature of the
discourses supplied by biomedical systems of knowledge and political
processes, which affect perceptions of aging. Both biomedical and political developments are uneven, ambivalent, and subject to elision, which
means that it is quite possible for different medical and political discourses of aging to coexist in different parts of the postmodern social
system.

Each generates a discourse that can legitimate the lives of older people
in particular ways, and as their influence accumulates, create the potential of entering into diverse discursive streams (Powell 2001a; Powell and
Edwards 2002). Medical and political discourses contribute to a subterranean coherence, which may help to explain their coexistence. Each offers a view of aging while downloading "risk" and uploading "responsibility" onto aging subjects (Biggs and Powell 2001; Powell 2001d).

A further critical reflection centers on the extent of subjectivity afforded
to people in later life. It can be suggested that this includes at least two
factors key to the process of aging: (1) the creation of spaces in which to
perform "consumer" roles and be recognized as consumers, as well as to
have intervention when "risk" can be "seen"; (2) the supply of material

with which "technologies of self" can flourish without being dominated by biomedical knowledge and professional power (Powell 2001e; Powell and Edwards 2002). Indeed, it can be argued that a modernist narrative of "decline" through postmodern "consumer aging" could coexist, with one emphasizing biomedical surveillance of objects of knowledge while the other highlights self-subjectification, and self-actualization.

Aging is a site upon which power is distributed and "power/knowledge" (cf. Powell 2001a) relations are played out, mainly through narratives engaged at the interpersonal level between subjects/objects of knowledge and professional experts. It is suggested, then, that:

> narratives of aging are personal insofar as we apply techniques to ourselves, while the technologies and the ground on which they are told imply particular distributions of power that will determine the way and the what of the storyline. (Biggs and Powell 2001, 113)

Discourses of aging therefore provide narrative prototypes within which certain categories of persons or groups are encouraged to live out their lives. This performativity may differ significantly from an individual's or group's everyday experience and requires a critical understanding of the postmodern with emphasis on localistic analyses of embodiment, subjectivity, and risk.

References

Achenbaum, A. W. 1978. *Old Age in the New Land*. Baltimore: John Hopkins University Press.

Age Concern England. 1997. *Age Matters: Report on a National Gallup Survey*. London: ACE.

Alcock, P. 1996. *Social Policy in Britain: Themes and Issues*. Basingstoke: Macmillan.

Arber, S., and J. Ginn. 1991. *Gender and Later Life: A Sociological Analysis of Resources and Constraints*. London: Sage.

Arber, S., and J. Ginn, eds. 1995. *Connecting Gender and Ageing: A Sociological Approach*. Milton Keynes, U.K.: Oxford University Press.

Armstrong, D. 1983. *The Political Anatomy of the Body*. Cambridge: Cambridge University Press.

Baltes, B., and M. F. Baltes. 1990. *Successful Aging: Perspectives from the Behavioural Sciences*. New York: Cambridge University Press.

Baltes, M., and L. Carstersen. 1996. "The Process of Successful Ageing." *Ageing and Society* 16:397–422.

Bauman, Z. 1992. *Imitations of Postmodernity*. London: Routledge.

———. 2001. *The Individualized Society*. Cambridge: Polity.

Beck, U. 1986. *Risikogesellschaft. Auf dem Weg in eine andere Moderne*. Frankfurt am Main: Suhrkamp.

———. 1992. *Risk Society: Towards a New Modernity*. London: Sage.

———. 1994. "The Reinvention of Politics: Towards a Theory of Reflexive Modernization." In *Reflexive Modernization: Politics, Tradition and Aesthetics in the Modern Social Order*, edited by U. Beck, A. Giddens, and S. Lash, 1–55. Stanford, Calif.: Stanford University Press.

Bengston, V., E. Burgess, and T. Parrot. 1997. "Theory, Explanation and a Third Generation of Theoretical Development in Social Gerontology." *Journal of Gerontology: Social Sciences* 52 (B): 72–88.

Bengtson, V., and R. Schaie. 1999. *Handbook of Theories in Gerontology.* New York: Springer.

Best, F. 1980. *Flexible Life Scheduling.* New York: Praeger.

Biggs, S. 1993. *Understanding Ageing.* Milton Keynes, U.K.: Oxford University Press.

———. 1996. "A Family Concern: Elder Abuse in British Social Policy." *Critical Social Policy* 16 (2): 63–88.

———. 1999. *The Mature Imagination.* Milton Keynes, U.K.: Oxford University Press.

Biggs, S., and J. L. Powell. 2000. "Surveillance and Elder Abuse: The Rationalities and Technologies of Community Care." *Journal of Contemporary Health* 4 (1): 43–49.

———. 2001. "A Foucauldian Analysis of Old Age and the Power of Social Welfare." *Journal of Aging & Social Policy* 12 (2): 93–111.

———. 2002. "Older People and Family Policy: A Critical Narrative." In *International Perspectives on the Family,* edited by V. Bengston and A. Lowenstein. Thousand Oaks, Calif.: Pine Forge Press.

Blaikie, A. 1999. *Ageing and Popular Culture.* Cambridge: Cambridge University Press.

Bond, J., and P. Coleman. 1990. *Ageing in Society.* London: Sage.

Bone, M. 1996. *Trends in Dependency among Older People in England.* London: Office of Population and Census Statistics.

Boneham, M., and K. Blakemore. 1994. *Age, Race and Ethnicity.* Buckingham: Oxford University Press.

Bornat, J., et al., eds. 1993. *Community Care: A Reader.* Milton Keynes, U.K.: Oxford University Press.

Bowl, R. 1986. "Social Work with Old People." In *Ageing and Social Policy,* edited by C. Phillipson and A. Walker. London: Gower.

Braidotti, R. 1994. *Nomadic Subjects. Embodiment and Sexual Difference in Contemporary Feminist Theory.* New York: Columbia University Press.

Burchell, G. 1993. "Liberal Government and the Techniques of the Self." *Economy and Society* 22 (3): 267–82.

Burchell, G., et al. 1991. *The Foucault Effect: Studies in Governmentality.* Hemel Hempstead: Harvester Wheatsheaf.

Bury, M. 1995. "Ageing, Gender and Sociological Theory." In *Connecting Gender and Ageing: A Sociological Approach,* edited by S. Arber and J. Ginn. Milton Keynes, U.K.: Oxford University Press.

Butler, J. 1987. *Bodies that Matter on the Discursive Limits of "Sex."* Oxford: Clarendon.

Bytheway, B. 1993. "Ageing and Biography: The Letters of Bernard and Mary Berenson." *Sociology* 27 (1): 153–65.

Bytheway, B., and J. Johnson. 1998. "The Sight of Age." In *The Body in Everyday Life*, edited by S. Nettleton and J. Watson, 62–85.

Bytheway, W. 1995. *Ageism*. Milton Keynes, U.K.: Oxford University Press.

Cabinet Office UK. 1998. *Better Government for Older People*. London: H.M.S.O.

Calasanti, T. M. 1996. "Incorporating Diversity: Meaning, Levels of Research, and Implications for Theory." *The Gerontologist* 36 (2): 147–56.

Cassel, E. J. 1991. *The Nature of Suffering and the Goals of Medicine*. New York: Oxford University Press.

Castel, R. 1991. "From Dangerousness to Risk." In *The Foucault Effect: Studies in Governmentality*, edited by G. Burchell, C. Gordon, and P. Miller. London: Harvester/Wheatsheaf:281–98.

Chau, W. F. 1995. "Experts, Networks and Inscriptions in the Fabrication of Accounting Images." *Accounting Organisations and Society* 20 (2/3): 111–45.

Christian, B. 1996. *"The Race for Theory."* In *Radically Speaking: Feminism Reclaimed*, edited by D. Bell and R. Klein. London: Zed Books.

Chudacoff, H. 1989. *How Old Are You?* Princeton, N.J.: Princeton University Press.

Clough, R. 1988. *Practice, Politics and Power in Social Service Departments*. Aldershot, U.K.: Gower.

Clough, R., and C. Hadley. 1996. *Care in Chaos*. London: Cassel.

Cohen, S. 1985. *Visions of Social Control*. Cambridge: Polity.

Cole, T., D. Van Tassel, and R. Kastenbaum. (1992). *Handbook of the Humanities and Aging*. New York: Springer.

Connor, S. 1989. *Postmodernist Culture*. Oxford: Basil Blackwell.

Conrad, S. 1992. "Old Age in the Modern and Postmodern Western World." In *Handbook of the Humanities and Aging*, edited by T. Cole. New York: Springer Publishing Company.

Cook, I. G. 2001. *A Human Geography of China*. London: Curzon.

Cook, I. G., and G. Murray. 2000. *China's Third Revolution: Tensions in the Transition to Post-Communism*. London: Curzon.

Cook, I. G., and J. L. Powell. 2003. "Active Aging in China." *Journal of Social Sciences and Humanities* 26 (2): 1–10.

Cousins, M., and A. Hussain. 1984. *Michel Foucault*. London: Macmillan.

Cumming, E., and W. Henry. 1961. *Growing Old: The Process of Disengagement*. New York: Basic Books.

Dalley, G. 1988. *Ideologies of Caring*. London: Macmillan.

Davidson, A. 1986. "Archaeology, Genealogy, Ethics." In *Foucault: A Critical Reader*, edited by D. Hoy. Oxford: Basil Blackwell.

Deakin, N. 1996. "The Devil's in the Detail: Some Reflections on Contracting for Social Care." *Social Policy and Administration* 30 (1): 20–38.

Delanty, G. 1999. *Social Science: Beyond Constructivism*. London: Sage.

Derrida, J. 1978. *Writing and Difference*. Chicago: University of Chicago Press.

Donzelot, J. 1979. *The Policing of Families*. London: Hutchinson.

———. 1988. "The Promotion of the Social." *Economy and Society* 17 (3): 395–427.

Douglas, M. 1985. *Risk Acceptability According to the Social Sciences.* New York: Sage.

Dreyfus, H., and P. Rabinow. 1983. *Michel Foucault: Beyond Hermeneutics,* London: Tavistock.

Du Gay, P. 1996. *Consumption and Identity.* London: Sage.

Du, P., and P. Tu. 2000. "Population Ageing and Old Age Security." In *The Changing Population of China,* edited by X. Peng and Z. Guo, 77–90. Oxford: Blackwell.

Elder, G. 1977. *The Alienated: Growing Old Today.* London: Writers and Readers Publishing Co-operative.

Erikson, E. 1980. *Identity and the Life Cycle: A Re-issue.* New York: W. W. Norton.

Estes, C. 1979. *The Aging Enterprise.* San Francisco: Jossey-Bass.

Estes, C., J. Swan, and L. Gerard. 1982. "Dominant and Competing Paradigms in Gerontology: Towards a Political Economy of Ageing." *Ageing and Society* 12:151–64.

Estes, C., and E. A. Binney. 1989. "The Biomedicalization of Aging: Dangers and Dilemmas." *The Gerontologist* 29 (5): 587–96.

Estes, C., and Associates. 2001. *Social Policy and Aging.* Thousand Oaks, Calif.: Sage.

Estes, C., S. Biggs, and C. Phillipson. 2003. *Social Theory, Social Policy and Ageing.* Milton Keynes, U.K.: Oxford University Press.

Ewald, F. 1993. "Two Infinities of Risk." In *The Politics of Everyday Fear,* edited by B. Massumi. Minneapolis: University of Minnesota Press.

Fattah, E. A., and V. F. Sacco. 1989. *Crime and Victimisation of the Elderly.* New York: Springer.

Featherstone, M., and M. Hepworth. 1993. "Images in Ageing." In *Ageing in Society,* edited by J. Bond, P. Coleman, and S. Peace. London: Sage.

Featherstone, M., and A. Wernick. 1995. *Images of Ageing.* London: Routledge.

Fennell, G., et al. 1988. *Sociology of Age.* Buckingham: Oxford University Press.

Finch, J. 1986. "Age." In *Key Variables in Social Investigation,* edited by R. Burgess. London: Routledge & Kegan Paul.

Flynn, R. 1992. *Structures of Control in Health Management.* London: Routledge.

———. 2002. "Clinical Governance and Governmentality." *Health, Risk & Society* 4 (2): 155–73.

Fortes, M. 1984. "Age, Generation and Social Structure." In *Age and Anthropological Theory,* edited by D. Kertzer and J. Keith. London: Cornell University Press.

———. 1967. *Madness and Civilisation.* London: Tavistock.

———. 1972. *The Archaeology of Knowledge.* London: Tavistock.

———. 1973. *The Birth of the Clinic.* London: Routledge.

———. 1976. *The History of Sexuality.* Harmondsworth: Penguin.

———. 1977. *Discipline and Punish.* London: Tavistock.

———. 1978. "Governmentality." In *The Foucault Effect*, edited by G. Burchell, C. Gordon, and P. Miller (1991).

———. 1980. *Power/Knowledge: Selected Interviews and Other Writings, 1972–1977*. New York: Pantheon.

———. 1982. "The Subject of Power." In *Michel Foucault: Beyond Structuralism and Hermeneutics*, edited by H. Dreyfus and P. Rabinow. Brighton, U.K.: Harvester.

———. 1988. "Technologies of the Self." In *Technologies of the Self*, edited by L. H. Martin, et al. London: Tavistock.

Frank, A. W. 1990. "Bringing Bodies Back In: A Decade Review." *Theory, Culture & Society* 7 (1): 131–62.

———. 1991. "For a Sociology of the Body: An Analytical Review." In *The Body Social Processes and Cultural Theory*, edited by M. Featherstone, M. Hepworth, and B. Turner. London: Sage.

———. 1996. *The Wounded Storyteller: Body, Illness and Ethics*. Chicago: University of Chicago Press.

Fraser, N. 1987. "Women, Welfare and the Politics of Need Interpretation." *Hytapia: A Journal of Feminist Philosophy* 2:102–21.

Freund, P. 1988. "Bringing Society into the Body: Understanding Socialized Human Nature." *Theory and Society* 17:839–64.

Friedan, B. 1993. *The Fountain of Age*. London: Cape Books.

Fullmer, E. M. 1995. "Challenging Biases against Families of Older Gays and Lesbians." In *Strengthening Aging Families: Diversity in Practice and Policy*, edited by G. C. Smith, S. S. Tobin, et al., 99–119. Thousand Oaks, Calif.: Sage.

Garland, D. 1985. *Punishment and Welfare*. Aldershot, U.K.: Gower.

George, L. 1995. "The Last Half-Century of Aging Research—and Thoughts for the Future." *Journal of Gerontology: Social Sciences* 50 (B) (1): 1–3.

Giddens, A. 1987. *Social Theory and Modern Sociology*. Cambridge: Polity.

———. 1990. *The Consequences of Modernit*. Cambridge: Polity.

———. 1991. *Modernity and Self- Identity: Self and Society in the Late Modern Age*. Cambridge: Polity.

Gilleard, C., and P. Higgs. 2000. *Cultures of Ageing*. London: Prentice-Hall.

Gittens, C. 1997. *The Pursuit of Beauty*. London: NPG.

Gordon, C. 1991. "Governmental Rationality: An Introduction." In *The Foucault Effect*, edited by G. Burchell, C. Gordon, and P. Miller, 1–51. Chicago: Chicago University Press.

Granovetter, M. 1985. "Economic Action and Social Structure—The Problem of Embeddedness." *American Journal of Sociology* 91 (3): 481–510.

———. 1992. "Economic Institutions as Social Constructions," *Acta Sociologica* 25 (3): 3–11.

Greenblatt, S. 1980. *Renaissance Self-Fashioning: From More to Shakespeare*. Chicago: Chicago University Press.

Grosz, E. 1994. *Volitile Bodies*. Bloomington: Indiana University Press.

Gutting, G., ed. 1994. *The Cambridge Companion to Foucault*. Cambridge: Cambridge University Press.

Habermas, J. 1981. *The Theory of Communicative Action*. London: Beacon Press.

———. 1984. *The Philosophical Discourse of Modernity*. Cambridge: Polity.

———. 1992. *Postmetaphysical Thinking*. Cambridge: Polity.

Hacking, I. 1990. *The Taming of Chance*. Cambridge: Cambridge University Press.

Hall, S., ed. 1992. *Modernity and Its Futures*. Cambridge: Polity.

Hallam, E., J. Hockey, and G. Howarth. 1999. *Beyond the Body: Death and Social Identity*. London: Routledge.

Haraway, D. 1991. *Simians, Cyborgs and Women*. London: Free Association Books.

Harper, S., and G. Laws. 1995. "Rethinking the Geography of Ageing." *Progress in Human Geography* 19 (2): 199–221.

Harper, S. 1997. "Constructing Later Life/Constructing the Body: Some Thoughts from Feminist Theory." In *Critical Approaches to Ageing and Later Life*, edited by A. Jamieson, S. Harper, and C. Victor, 160–71. Buckingham: Open University Press.

Hewitt, M. 1983. "Bio-politics and Social Policy: Foucault's Account of Welfare." *Theory, Culture and Society* 2 (1): 67–84.

Hirst, P. 1981. "The Genesis of the Social." *Politics and Power* 3:67–82.

Hockey, J. and A. James. 1993. *Growing Up and Growing Old: Ageing and Dependency in the Life Course*, London: Sage.

Howe, D. 1992. "Child Abuse and the Bureacratization of Social Work." *Sociological Review* 40 (3): 491–505.

Howe, A. 1994. *Punish and Critique: Towards a Feminist Analysis of Penality*. London: Routledge.

Hughes, B. 1995. *Older People and Community Care: Critical Theory and Practice*. Milton Keynes, U.K.: Oxford University Press.

Ignatieff, M. 1978. *A Just Measure of Pain*. London: Macmillan.

Ingleby, D. 1985. "Professionals as Socialisers: The 'Psy' Complex." In *Research in Law, Deviance and Social Control*, edited by A. Scully and S. Spitzer, 7.

Irvine, E. 1954. "Research into Problem Families." *British Journal of Psychiatric Social Work* 9 (Spring).

Isay, R. A. 1996. *Becoming Gay: The Journey to Self-acceptance*. New York: Pantheon Books.

Itzin, C. 1986. "Ageism Awareness Training: A Model for Group Work." In *Dependency and Interdependency in Old Age: Theoretical Perspectives and Policy Alternatives*, edited by C. Phillipson, M. Bernard, and P. Strang. London: Croom Helm.

Jameson, F. 1991. *Postmodernism, or, the Cultural Logic of Late Capitalism*. London: Verso.

Jefferys, M., and P. Thane. 1989. "An Ageing Society and Ageing People." In *Growing Old in the Twentieth Century*, edited by M. Jefferys. London: Routledge.

Johnson, T. 1995. "Governmentality and the Institutionalisation of Expertise." In *Health Professions and the State in Europe*, edited by G. Larkin, et al. London: Routledge.

Jones, C. 1983. *State Social Work and the Working Class*. London: Macmillan.

Kalish, R. 1979. "The New Ageism and the Failure Models: A Polemic." *The Gerontologist* 19 (4).

Katz, S. 1996. *Disciplining Old Age: The Formation of Gerontological Knowledge*, Charlottesville: University Press of Virginia.

———. 1999. "Lifecourse, Lifestyle and Postmodern Culture: Corporate Representations of Later Life," paper presented at Restructuring Work and the Lifecourse: An International Symposium, Institute of Human Development, University of Toronto.

———. 2000. "Busy Bodies: Activity, Aging and the Management of Everyday Life." *Journal of Aging Studies* 14 (2): 135–52.

Kastenbaum, R. 1993. "Encrusted Elders." In *Voices & Visions of Aging*, edited by T. Cole. New York: Springer.

Krug, E. G. 2002. *World Report on Violence and Health*. Geneva: World Health Organisation.

Kunkel, S., and L. Morgan. 1999. *Aging: The Social Context*. New York: Pine Forge.

Leonard, P. 1997. *Postmodern Welfare*. London: Sage.

Longino, C. F. 1994. "Pressure from Our Aging Population Will Broaden Our Understanding of Medicine." *Academic Medicine* 72 (10): 841–47.

Longino, C. F., and J. L. Powell. 2004. "Embodiment and the Study of Aging." In *The Body in Human Inquiry: Interdisciplinary Explorations of Embodiment*, edited by V. Berdayes. New York: Hampton Press.

Lubove, R. 1966. "Social Work and the Life of the Poor." *The Nation*, 23 May, 609–11.

Luhmann, N. 1993. *Risk: A Sociological Theory*. Berlin: Walter de Gruyter.

Lupton, D. 1999. *Risk*. New York: Routledge.

Lyotard, J. F. 1984. *The Postmodern Condition: A Report on Knowledge*. Manchester, U.K.: Manchester University Press.

Massumi, B., ed. 1993. *The Politics of Everyday Fear*. Minneapolis: University of Minnesota Press.

May, T. 1996. *Situating Social Theory*. Milton Keynes, U.K.: Oxford University Press.

McAdams, D. 1993. *The Stories We Live By*. New York: Morrow.

McLennan, G. 1992. "The Enlightenment Project Revisited." In *Modernity and Its Futures*, edited by S. Hall, D. Held, and T. McGrew. Cambridge: Polity.

Miller, J. 1993. *The Passion of Michel Foucault*. New York: Simon & Schuster.

Mills, C. W. 1959. *The Sociological Imagination*. London: Penguin.

Minkler, M., and C. Estes, eds. 1998. *Critical Gerontology: Perspectives from Political and Moral Economy*. New York: Baywood.

Mölling, G. 2001. "The Nature of Trust: From George Simmel to a Theory of Expectation, Interpretation and Suspension." *Sociology* 35 (2): 403–20.

Moody, H. 1998. *Aging, Concepts and Controversies*. Thousand Oaks, Calif.: Pine Forge Press, Sage.

Morris, D. B. 1991. *The Culture of Pain*. London: University of California Press.

———. 1998. *Illness and Culture in the Postmodern Age*. London: University of California Press.

Mouzelis, N. 1991. *Back to Sociological Theory*. London: Macmillan.

Murphy, J. W., and C. F. Longino Jr. 1997. "Reason, the Lifeworld, and Appropriate Intervention." *Journal of Applied Gerontology* 16 (2): 149–51.

Neugarten, B. L. 1974. "Age Groups in American Society and the Rise of the Young-old." *Annals of the American Academy of Political and Social Sciences* 415: 187–98.

Neugarten, D., ed. 1996. *The Meanings of Age*. Chicago: University of Chicago Press.

Oberg, P., and L. Tornstam. 1999. "Body Images among Men and Women of Different Ages." *Ageing and Society* 19:645–58.

Pain, R. 2003. "Old Age and Victimisation." In *Victimisation, Theory, Research and Policy*, edited by P. Davis, et al. London: Macmillan.

Patel, N. 1990. *A Race against Time*. London: Runnymede Trust.

Phillipson, C. 1982. *Capitalism and the Construction of Old Age*. London: Macmillan.

———. 1988. "Challenging Dependency: Towards a New Social Work with Older People." In *Radical Social Work Today*, edited by M. Langan and P. Lee. London: Unwin Hyman.

———. 1998. *Reconstructing Old Age*. London: Sage.

Phillipson, C., and A. Walker, eds. 1986. *Ageing and Social Policy: A Critical Assessment*. Aldershot, U.K.: Gower.

Phillipson, C., and S. Biggs. 1998. "Modernity and Identity: Themes and Perspectives in the Study of Older Adults." *Journal of Aging and Identity* 3 (1): 11–23.

Phillipson, C., and J. L. Powell. 2004. "Risk, Social Welfare and Old Age." In *Old Age and Human Agency*, edited by E. Tulle. Hauppauge, N.Y.: Nova Science Publishers.

Powell, J. L. 1998. "The "Us" and the "Them": Connecting Political Economy and Foucauldian Insights into Ageing Bodies." 1–25, paper presented to the British Sociological Association Annual Conference, University of Edinburgh.

———. 1999. Review of S. Katz (1996), "Disciplining Old Age: The Formation of Gerontological Knowledge." *Canadian Journal of Sociology* 55 (3): 45–48.

———. 2000. "The Importance of a 'Critical' Sociology of Old Age." *Social Science Paper Publisher* 3 (1): 1–5.

———. 2001a. "The NHS and Community Care Act 1990 in the United Kingdom: A Critical Review between the Years 1981 to 1996." *Sincronia: Journal of Social Sciences and Humanities* 4 (4): 1–10.

———. 2001b. "Social Theory and the Aging Body." *International Journal of Language, Society and Culture* 8 (2): 1–10.

———. 2001c. "Aging and Social Theory: A Sociological Review." *Social Science Paper Publisher* 4 (2): 1–12.

———. 2001d. "Theorizing Gerontology: The Case of Old Age, Professional Power and Social Policy in the United Kingdom." *Journal of Aging & Identity* 6 (3): 117–35.

———. 2001e. "Rethinking Structure and Agency: Bio-ethics, Aging and Technologies of the Self." *Sincronia: Journal of Social Sciences and Humanities* 4 (4): 1–10.

———. 2001f. "Women in British Special Hospitals: A Sociological Approach." *Sincronia: Journal of Social Sciences and Humanities* 4 (4): 1–14.

———. 2002. "Archaeology and Genealogy: Developments in Foucauldian Gerontology." *Sincronia: Journal of Social Sciences and Humanities* 5 (1): 1–10.

Powell, J. L., and S. Biggs. 2000. "Managing Old Age: The Disciplinary Web of Power, Surveillance and Normalisation." *Journal of Aging and Identity* 5 (1): 3–13.

———. 2003. "Foucauldian Gerontology." *Electronic Journal of Sociology* 7 (3): 1–11.

———. 2004. "Aging, Technologies of Self, and Bio-Medicine: A Foucauldian Excursion." *International Journal of Sociology and Social Policy* 23 (13): 96–115.

Powell, J. L., and I. Cook. 2000. "'A Tiger Behind and Coming Up Fast': Governmentality and the Politics of Population Control in China." *Journal of Aging & Identity* 5 (2): 79–90.

———. 2001. "Understanding Foucauldian Philosophy: The Case of the Chinese State and the Surveillance of Older People." *International Journal of Language, Society and Culture* 8 (1): 1–9.

Powell, J. L., and J. L. Edwards. 2002. "Policy Narratives of Aging: The Right Way, the Third Way or the Wrong Way?" *Electronic Journal of Sociology* 6 (1): 1–9.

Powell, J. L., and C. F. Longino. 2001. "Towards the Postmodernization of Aging: the Body and Social Theory." *Journal of Aging & Identity* 6 (4): 20–34.

———. 2002. "Modernism v. Postmodernism: Rethinking Theoretical Tensions in Social Gerontology." *Journal of Aging Studies* 7 (4): 115–25.

Powell, J. L., and M. M. Edwards. 2003. "Risk and Youth: A Critical Sociological Narrative." *International Journal of Sociology and Social Policy* 23 (12): 81–95.

Powell, J. L., and A. Wahidin. 2003. "Re-configuring Old Bodies: From the Biomedical Model to a Critical Epistemology." *Journal of Social Sciences and Humanities* 26 (2): 1–10.

———. 2004. "Corporate Crime, Aging and Pensions in Great Britain." *Journal of Societal and Social Policy* 3 (1): 37–55.

Rabinow, P., ed. 1984. *The Foucault Reader*. London: Peregrine.

Reddy, S. 1996. "Claims to Expert Knowledge and the Subversion of Democracy: The Triumph of Risk over Uncertainty." *Economy and Society* 25 (2): 222–54.

Rose, N. 1993. "Government, Authority, and Expertise in Advanced Liberalism." *Economy and Society* 22 (3): 283–99.

———. 1996. "The Death of the Social? Refiguring the Territory of Government." *Economy and Society* 25 (3): 237–56.

Rose, N., and P. Miller. 1992. "Political Power Beyond the State: Problematics of Government." *British Journal of Sociology* 43 (2): 172–205.

Saraga, E., ed. 1998. *Embodying the Social: Constructions of Difference*. London: Routledge.

Satyamurti, C. 1974. "Women's Occupation and Social Change: The Case of Social Work." Paper presented to 1974 British Sociological Association's Annual Conference.

Scarfe, G. 1993. *Scarface*. London: Sinclaire-Stevenson.

Schrag, P. 1980. *Mind Control*. New York: Marion Bowyars.

Seidman, S. 1994. *Contested Knowledge: Social Theory in the Postmodern Era*. Oxford: Blackwell.

Shilling, C. 1993. *The Body & Social Theory*. London: Sage.

Shumway, D. 1989. *Michel Foucault*. Charlottesville: University Press of Virginia.

Sim, J., et al., eds. 1987. *Law, Order and the Authoritarian State*. Milton Keynes, U.K.: Oxford University Press.

Smart, B. 1985. *Michel Foucault*. London: Routledge.

———. 1993. *Postmodernity*. London: Routledge.

Sontag, S. 1978. "The Double Standard of Ageing." In *An Ageing Population*, edited by V. Carver and P. Liddiard.Milton Keynes, U.K.: Oxford University Press.

———. 1991. *Illness as Metaphor and AIDS and Its Metaphors*. London: Penguin.

Steuerman, E. 1992. "Habermas vs. Lyotard: Modernity vs. Postmodernity?" In *Judging Lyotard*, edited by A. Benjamin. London: Routledge.

Stott, M. 1981. *Ageing for Beginners*. Oxford: Blackwell.

Thompson, E. P. 1967. "Time, Work—Discipline and Industrial Capitalism." *Past and Present* 38:56–97.

Thompson, K. 1992. "Social Pluralism and Postmodernity." In *Modernity and Its Futures*, edited by S. Hall, D. Held, and T. McGrew. Cambridge: Polity.

Timiras, P., ed. 1997. *Physiological Basis of Aging and Geriatrics*. 2nd ed. Paris: Masson.

Tinker, A. 1997. *Older People in Modern Society*. London: Longman.

Townsend, P. 1981. "The Structured Dependency of the Elderly: A Creation of Social Policy in the Twentieth Century." *Ageing and Society* 1 (1): 5–28.

Townsend, P., and D. Wedderburn. 1965. *The Aged in the Welfare State*. London: Bell.

Tulle-Winton, E. 1999. "Growing Old and Resistance: Towards a New Cultural Economy of Old Age?" *Ageing and Society* 19:281–99.

Tulloch, J., and D. Lupton. 2003. *Risk and Everyday Life*. London: Sage.

Turner, B. S. 1989. "Ageing, Status Politics and Sociological Theory." *British Journal of Sociology* 40:588–606.

———. 1995. "Ageing and Identity." In *Images of Ageing*, edited by M. Featherstone and A. Wernick. London: Routledge.

Twigg, J. 2000. "Social Policy and the Body." In *Rethinking Social Policy*, edited by G. Lewis, S. Gewirtz, and J. Clarke. London: Sage.

Veyne, P. 1980. *Foucault revolutionne l'histoire*. Paris: Éditions Seuil.

Victor, C. 1987. *Old Age in Modern Society*. London: Croom Helm.

Vincent, J. 1996. *Inequality and Old Age*. London: University College London Press.

Vincent, J. 1999. *Politics, Power and Old Age*. Buckingham: Open University Press.

Virilio, P. 1983. *Pure War*. New York: Semiotext.

Visker, R. 1995. *Michel Foucault*. Verso: London.

Wahidin, A., and J. L. Powell. 2001. "The Loss of Aging Identity: Social Theory, Old Age and the Power of Special Hospitals." *Journal of Aging & Identity* 6 (1): 31–49.

———. 2003. "Reconfiguring Old Bodies: From the Biomedical Model to a Critical Epistemology." *Journal of Social Sciences and Humanities* 26 (2): 1–10.

Walker, A. 1981. "Towards a Political Economy of Old Age." *Ageing and Society* 1:73–94.

———. 1985. *The Care Gap: How Can Local Authorities Meet the Needs of the Elderly?* London: Local Government Information Unit.

———. 1987. "The Social Construction of Dependency in Old Age." In *The State or the Market?* edited by M. Loney, 41–57. London: Sage.

———. 1990. "Poverty and Inequality in Old Age." In *Ageing and Society*, edited by J. Bond and P. Coleman. London: Sage.

Walker, A., and G. Naeghele. 1999. *The Politics of Old Age in Europe*. Milton Keynes, U.K.: Oxford University Press.

Warnes, A., ed. 1996. *Human Ageing and Later Life*. London: Edward Arnold.

Wilkinson, I. 2001. "Social Theories of Risk Perception: At Once Indispensable and Insufficient." *Current Sociology* 49 (1): 1–22.

Williams, F. 1994. *Social Policy: A Critical Introduction*, 2nd ed. Oxford: Blackwell.

Wynne, B. 1987. *Risk Management and Hazardous Waste*. Berlin: Springer.

Index